MW01473146

Best wishes
Robert

Excelerating

*Compared to what we ought to be,
 most of us are only half awake.
We are making use of only a small part of
 our possible mental and physical resources.*

—William James

Robert K. Cooper

Excelerating

Speeding Through Challenges

with Calm Effectiveness

in Leadership and Life

Advanced Excellence Systems LLC
c/o Services for Success, Inc.
P.O. Box 7566
Des Moines, IA 50322
515-278-1700
www.RobertKCooper.com

Copyright © 2002 by Advanced Excellence Systems LLC

All rights reserved. No part of this book may be reproduced or transmitted in any form or by any means, electronic or mechanical, including photocopying, recording, or by any information storage and retrieval system, without permission in writing from the publisher.

Published by Advanced Excellence Systems LLC.
www.RobertKCooper.com

Excelerating is a service mark of Advanced Excellence Systems LLC.

Printed in the United States of America.

Library of Congress Control Number: 2002091535

Cooper, Robert K.
  Excelerating: speeding through challenges with calm effectiveness in leadership and life
  Robert K. Cooper – 1st ed.
Includes biographical references.

1. Self-actualization (Psychology)
2. Success – Psychological aspects
I. Title: Excelerating

ISBN 0-9719832-1-6

10 9 8 7 6 5 4 3 2 1
First Edition

To all who realize that
the next frontier is not only in front of us,
it's also inside of us.

To my family:
My wife, Leslie
My children, Chris, Chelsea, and Shanna
My parents, Hugh and Margaret Cooper
My grandmothers, Nora Roby Cooper and Marion Downing
My grandfathers, Hugh Cooper, Sr., and Wendell L. Downing, M.D.
Who alone or together
Showed me worlds I never knew.

It is useless to close the gates against new ideas; they overleap them.

—Wenzel Lothar Metternich

Contents

Preface: Swimming Through Fire 9

Introduction: The Gift of Obstacles...15

Chapter 1: Toughen Up 25

Chapter 2: Calm Down 45

Chapter 3: See Near *and* Far 55

Chapter 4: Improvise..67

Chapter 5: Adapt..79

Chapter 6: Overcome 93

Final Thoughts: When Your Moment Comes...107

Acknowledgements 111

Notes 113

About the Author 123

Contact Page...127

Preface

Swimming Through Fire

In a dark time, the eye begins to see.
—Theodore Roethke

Looking back, I remember one of the first experiences that sparked my lifelong interest in understanding why some people overcome adversity and so many others are thwarted by it. It was on a warm summer day in 1963, on a narrow dirt road framed by tall trees near Lake LaSalle, in Minnesota.

"We lived here a long time ago," my Grandfather Cooper told me as we walked. A narrow part of the river, perhaps thirty feet wide and only seven or eight feet deep in spots, ran beside us. The water moved fast and cold.

My grandfather walked with the aid of a cane. He was slowed by the aftereffects of three heart attacks he had survived, and the lingering limitations from a broken back in an automobile accident caused by a drunk driver. In pain and frustrated by his inability to do many of the things he had always loved, he often was very gruff with the people around him. But I saw another side of him, too. As the first grandchild, I pestered him with questions and kept asking to follow him around. At my urging, he talked about life and its lessons in ways that he may not have been able to talk with others. A light would come into his blue eyes when he would stop to tell me a story like this one, and for a time his ailments and disappointments seemed to melt away.

"Your grandmother and I loved to walk here," my grandfather said as he pointed things out to me. "Along the path past the old dam. You could hear the water moving fast once it cleared the dam. We loved to smell the pines and hear the wind rustling the trees. I still do."

He looked at me for a few moments, perhaps confirming to himself that I was old enough to hear what he was about to say. Or, perhaps he was reassuring himself that I would understand what he was about to tell me not as a tale of heroism, but as a deeply felt lesson about living life.

He continued, "We were out walking one summer evening. There had been some big fires nearby, but it had just rained that afternoon, so we weren't worried…" His voice trailed off as he caught his breath and recalled that day. "Then I smelled smoke. We turned around and saw the flames coming over that hill. A wall of flames—it was at least a hundred feet high. It crossed the rise and came down that slope toward us."

"The smoke rode ahead of the flames. It seemed like the whole world was suddenly on fire. Trees were snapping in two from the winds that the flames were generating. The air was filled with red-hot cinders, popping and sizzling. I grabbed your grandmother's arm. I was afraid. At first, I thought we could outrun it…" He swept his gaze across the line where the fire had come. "…but the next thing I knew, it was right behind us."

"I yelled to your grandmother to get into the water. She couldn't swim. 'Hold on to me!' I told her. I had no sense of time. A strange calm came over me. The heat was hitting us like waves from a huge oven. It was hard to breathe." I watched my grandfather, his hands trembling, remembering it all. "I tried to sense a gap in the heat, an opening, anything. I splashed water on us. Your grandmother didn't say a word. Just held on."

"Then the fire to the north of us jumped the water. It came on that roaring wind right across the river through the air above us, from the treetops on one side, to the ones on the other. You could hear the tops of the pines exploding as the fire took them."

"I pushed us away from the banks and started swimming low in the water as the flames went above us. That water was freezing cold and its surface was as red as the fire itself. I yelled to duck under the water. I'll never forget the look in her eyes…but she did it. That's your grandmother. She could be very strong." He chuckled and lightly shook his head as he said that, yet his eyes were blurred with tears and his voice was thick as he spoke. "We came up for air and went under again. I kept kicking to go deeper, and she seemed to be kicking right along with me. When we came up again, it was still hot and smoky but the fire was moving on."

"We got back to shore and walked home, shivering from fear and from our cold wet clothes. The fire had missed our little barn and house. That was a blessing. We held each other in front of the woodstove until we got warm."

"The next day we walked the fire line. Fifty feet to one side of that line and fifty feet to the other, not a thing was burned. Fire is like that, Robert. You can be standing just outside its reach and wonder how you're so lucky." He paused again. "Or maybe it comes over the top of you and you survive. My neighbor told someone at the local newspaper how we survived by swimming through the fire. I got all the credit in the paper,[1] but your grandmother was the truly brave one. I was just acting on instinct and I was doing things I knew how to do. Right there, on the spot, she had to conquer some of her worst fears. Otherwise, we wouldn't have made it. I wouldn't have left her behind."

He looked at me and asked me the kind of question he would always ask: "If you were standing right here and a fire came, what would you do?"

* * *

My grandfather only mentioned that experience again when I would ask him about it. He said it had happened long ago and there was nothing heroic about it: he had faced something unexpected and had done what he had to do, and it turned out all right. Every family and organization encounters times that call for direct, courageous action, he would say, and people are called to quietly and resolutely do whatever they can, with whatever they have at hand. Once, when I talked to my grandmother about this experience, there were tears in her eyes and she said, "It wasn't the worst thing we had to go through."

I later learned that the fire beside the river had followed a much greater adversity in my grandparents' lives—the death of their first child at birth, in my grandfather's arms as the country doctor stood beside him, unable to do anything to save the newborn boy. And then not long afterwards, someone set fire to my grandparents' home when they were away, and they lost everything.

So, although swimming through fire was not the hardest thing my grandparents ever faced, learning about it meant a lot to me. We don't succeed *despite* life's difficulties and challenges—we succeed *because* of them. Looking back, my grandfather didn't believe that challenges entered our lives to punish us, but rather to help us grow. There are times when, like it or not, we have to swim through fire.

The skills to do that are also the skills to better handle whatever other challenges, large or small, life may bring. How much better it would be, my grandfather realized, to build our readiness for adversity before we needed it, instead of counting on luck or willpower to pull us through.

I believe that this small book will help you do just that.

14   *Excelerating*

Introduction

The Gift of Obstacles

You can choose to go back toward safety or forward toward growth. Growth must be chosen again and again; fear must be overcome again and again.

—Abraham Maslow

These are tough times that call for tough people. The pace is fast, expectations and pressures keep rising, uncertainty and challenge are the orders of the day, and the sense of competition or feeling of threat sometimes seems like it's everywhere: at work, in schools—indeed, throughout the world. Even for those who are achieving success in their work and personal lives, there is often a feeling of loss—lost time, lost direction, lost connection to others and lost connection to personal values.

And yet, for thirty years, in a wide range of settings around the world, I have observed people of all ages and in all walks of life turn challenging times—and even extreme adversity—into the most satisfying kind of success. The kind of success that is consistent with their best and truest selves, that requires no sacrifice of what matters most to them, that brings them not just accomplishment in the eyes of society, but contentment in their own hearts.

In every community and organization, there are individuals who manage to rise above difficulty, uplift and encourage others, see farther ahead than the rest of us, seize hidden opportunities, stay cool in the face of overwhelming odds, act decisively when nothing seems certain, and improvise ways to advance when everyone else is turning away or giving up. Whenever I encounter these rare people, I ask myself three questions. The first is, "How do they do it?" The second is, "How can I do it" And the third is, "How might I help others to do it?"

My second question may sound selfish. It's not the kind of thing that researchers and advisors like myself often admit. But the truth is that I, perhaps like you, not only have a job, but also a family and personal passions and value-based commitments and a great desire for a full, satisfying life. So when I observe an idea that seems to work, or read about one, or devise a strategy based on others' research or my own, I first test it on myself and then apply it with my colleagues and groups in various situations. If it doesn't work well, I modify it—and then test it again. I am always searching for what I call "scientific shortcuts," the small proven tools that save time and increase results.

They are collected in this book: the best, simplest ways I have found to move through challenges, adversity, and stress toward your true priorities—and to do that quickly, amid the persistent pressures and demands of our modern life and work.

Each time you apply a technique or action from this book, you will learn how to do even better the next time: how to continue handling challenges with calm effectiveness while bringing out the finest qualities in yourself and those around you. Some of that learning is conscious, embodied in methods and strategies you can master and then apply again and again. Much of it goes on without you even being aware of it, because you are actually altering the brain and body pathways that govern large parts of your reactions to adversity.

At least in this way, that old saying is true: adversity can be the best teacher. If you use the tools in this book with self-awareness, responding to challenges and change in new ways, you will learn a lot about yourself. And you will also learn a lot—both consciously and at deeper levels in your brain and body—about how to handle challenges better the next time. And the time after that.

That's why I titled this book *Excelerating*. Because it not only helps you *excel*, it also teaches you how to *accelerate* your positive, constructive reactions to events and circumstance that might previously have bogged you down. Instead of tensing up, freaking out, or falling behind, you learn to turn adversity into success. You expand your future without threatening your foundation. You replace frantic rushing with calm effectiveness. You streamline your efforts, put priorities first, and return more rapidly to an even keel.

When you appreciate the value of excelerating, you shrug off the reasons you once had for going along, getting by, giving in, or turning away. You face the hardest and most unpredictable tests that life and work can deliver—as well as all the maddening little frustrations of everyday life—without wishing you were somewhere, or someone else. You set higher goals for yourself because you recognize that you have the inherent ability to reach them. You keep embracing what's essential and discarding the rest. You stretch the boundaries of the possible. Merely surviving or coping, which seem to be the goals too many people today have accepted for their stress-filled lives, is not nearly enough. So, applied at the right times, excelerating can be exhilarating, too.

Not just individuals, but teams and organizations perform best when they use excelerating skills. Research demonstrates that such skills help them succeed even when they encounter severe challenges.[2]

In case you're thinking that "excelerating" is little more than a semantic twist, here's my response: words matter, because what you call something affects how you react emotionally to it.[3] This particular word, excelerating, represents a different lens for knowing—and having—what it takes to triumph during times of constant change both on and off the job, and deciding for yourself what works, what doesn't, and why.

Excelerating is a learnable skill and an attitude that can be built into your life and work. Many of the insights and practical tools in this book take only moments to apply. I know they have worked for me, my family, and the many individuals and organizations that I have advised. I encourage you to put them to the test right away in your own unique circumstances, to begin turning adversity into progress, new strengths, and a lifelong sense of authentic fulfillment.

As illustrated below, there are six essential aspects of excelerating:

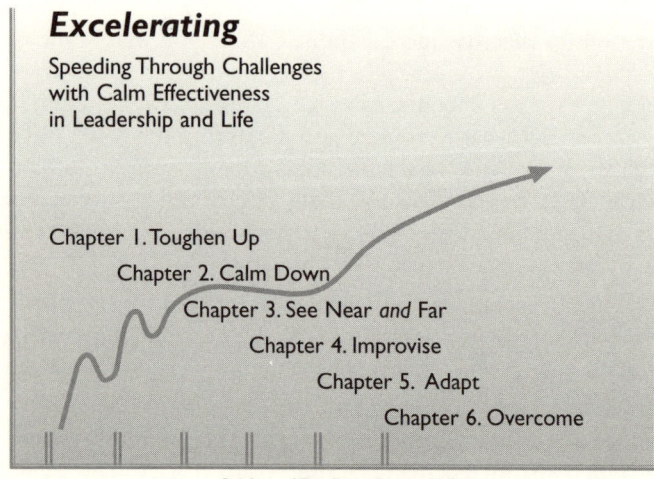

Excelerating

Speeding Through Challenges
with Calm Effectiveness
in Leadership and Life

Chapter 1. Toughen Up
Chapter 2. Calm Down
Chapter 3. See Near *and* Far
Chapter 4. Improvise
Chapter 5. Adapt
Chapter 6. Overcome

© Advanced Excellence Systems LLC
Web Site: www.RobertKCooper.com

The Six Aspects of Excelerating

Each of these aspects has value in its own right, and you can learn and practice them in any order according to your own preferences and needs. Here's how I define them:

- *Toughen Up*
    ...to build the inherent ability to make adversity your ally.
- *Calm Down*
    ...to respond with poised effectiveness to pressure and uncertainty.
- *See Near* and *Far*
    ...to pay exceptional attention to what's right in front of you, without losing sight of where you are trying to go.
- *Improvise*
    ...to create and enact your own best way forward.
- *Adapt*
    ...to adjust to new and varying conditions, learning as you go.
- *Overcome*
    ...to persevere and keep growing, giving the world the best you have.

Change Your Brain, Change Your Results

Surprisingly small shifts in the brain can change us greatly.
—Robert Ornstein, Ph.D.

When you use the techniques and methods in this book, you actually modify the structure of your brain, senses, and nervous system. You reorient the instantaneous, unconscious response patterns in your brain and body, replacing unproductive reactions with calm effectiveness. You also create constructive new habits to replace negative practices that keep you from being at your best and achieving better results.

Growing research evidence supports this claim, which I have also written about elsewhere.[4] It is not necessary for you to understand in detail the nature of that research or the actual workings of your brain, but I feel that it is important that you recognize your immense capacity for fundamental change, because it provides an important incentive to try out the actions and approaches I'm recommending. Even if things don't go perfectly the first or second time you try them, you are making yourself better for the third or fourth time.

Here's why. Whenever you respond to pressures, your mind, emotions, and body tend to follow the strongest pattern of your past habits. Scientists call this a facilitated pathway in the nervous system. If your past responses to pressure have been less than fully effective, your present and future ones almost certainly will be too. But, whenever you forego old habits and make small, specific, positive changes in your actions, you produce changes in the brain itself.[5]

There is a whole lot going on throughout your brain and body every time you respond to a challenge. Much of it has been programmed through millennia of evolution to protect you from danger—but *not* to help you do and be your best. That's why there's such great payoff from making the conscious effort to override and retrain those systems.

The brain is very capable of changing—throughout our lives it retains a vast capacity for modification in response to our choices and our experiences.[6] The psychologist Erik Erikson observed that there are times in every life when we must choose between stagnation and what he called *generativity*. As Dr. Paula Hardin explains that concept, "Generativity is a process that includes giving birth to the new aspects of ourselves that will assure a higher sense of well-being. It means finding new and practical ways of caring for those beyond the family, those who come after us. The path of generativity helps us to avoid the dangers of self-absorption and stagnation because we learn to live in new ways that will continually expand our hearts and horizons."[7]

Too many people see their lives in today's world in terms of simple survival, which is really a form of stagnation: "If I can just get through this week, or this afternoon, or this meeting..."

Even when we are feeling relatively comfortable with the ways we handle change and adversity, there may still be a nagging sense that we could do better. Trust that intuition. You *can* develop more calm effectiveness to speed you through change and challenges more easily and productively than ever before.

Skills + Rehearsal = Results

It's not really surprising that we don't always handle difficult situations as well as we could. Consider that the most exceptional people in many fields—athletes, teachers, leaders, and artists, for example—spend much more time rehearsing than they do performing. Whereas, for most people it's just the opposite: almost no time practicing, and most of their time performing.[8] In the rush to achieve goals, there is little attention to actually learning, in advance, better ways to live and lead. Research shows that successful change in behavior depends on practice. It takes serious rehearsal to build new skills, especially when the task involves overturning deeply ingrained patterns or habits.[9]

Fortunately, some of this practice requires only moments of focus at a time, rather than hours. For example, even just envisioning a new way to respond to a challenge activates the same brain cells that are required to perfectly perform that response.[10] Mentally rehearsing a new way of behaving in the face of adversity activates the prefrontal cortex, the brain area that coordinates information and translates it into specific actions.[11] Without attentive rehearsal, the brain's prefrontal cortex does not mobilize in advance, and despite your best intentions the brain will act out old, counterproductive routines instead. When you practice, you prepare the prefrontal cortex to activate *ahead of* a new action, and you will be better at accomplishing it.

Results Begin Right Now

You might choose to begin improving your excelerating skills with the next chapter, which shows you ways to prepare yourself mentally and physically for difficult circumstances. But you might also select any other part of this book that interests you and start by testing the advice there. Any of the small actions you read about can be put into practice right away. Once you experience the results, I believe you will be enthusiastic about trying more.

Over time you will find yourself acquiring and applying the qualities that Albert Schweitzer, the Nobel Prize-winning humanitarian, said that we all need in order to excel in the face of life's many challenges: "the skin of a rhino and the soul of an angel."[12]

Several Highlights of the Neuroscience of Excelerating

Although there are many parts of your brain that separately, or in combination, affect your responses to adversity, here are several of the most significant ones.

The *limbic system* is the seat of emotions in the mind.[13] It functions 80,000 times faster than the thinking brain's cerebral cortex.[14] Every second of your life, it influences how you perceive what's happening and how you react to it.

Inside the limbic system is the *amygdala*, which scans everything that happens from moment to moment, on the lookout to preserve your existing "autopilot" routines and react instantly to any change by signaling "Emergency!" and enacting full-blown change-avoidance.[15]

The *cingulate* is a central switching point in the brain that enables you to constantly assess sensory stimuli and change focuses. It guides your close-up attention and, at the same time, supports future-oriented thinking so that you can handle changing conditions.

The *basal ganglia* and *reticular activating system* (RAS) surround the limbic system and aid in the integration of your thoughts, feelings, and movement, helping to coordinate your reactions to events. The basal ganglia is involved with the formation of habit patterns and complex actions that are mobilized with little, if any, conscious awareness. If, for example, a person in front of you on the sidewalk stumbles and begins to fall, you instantly step forward and reach out your hand to catch them: that's the basal ganglia taking charge. The RAS sorts through the 100 million impulses that reach the brain every second, aiming to deflect the trivial and let the vital pass through to alert the mind.[16] The RAS is evolutionarily primed to magnify negative incoming messages and minimize positive ones.

Given the choice, the RAS always interprets things negatively. "Better safe than sorry" are the words it lives by. It can cause you to overreact to a casual comment or to assume the worst when another person is vague or seems unsupportive or hostile.

Other brain areas, including the prefrontal cortex, temporal lobes, and cerebellum, also affect how you respond to pressures. Even more amazing, it is becoming clear that we have not just one brain, but four of them: the one in our head plus highly-developed, sophisticated brains in the heart, spine, and gut.[17]

It is increasingly important to become familiar with new ways to use each of these unique sources of intelligence. Many of the insights and practical tools throughout the rest of this book are based on this new research.

1

Toughen Up

...to build the inherent ability to make adversity your ally.

What we nurture in ourselves will grow: that is nature's eternal law.
—Goethe

Most every morning as the sun was just coming up, my grandfather would sit at his desk and think about the day ahead. Much of what he knew, he had learned the hard way. In his life he had been a surveyor, a detective, a minister, a teacher, and a school superintendent. He had suffered a number of debilitating injuries and experienced many setbacks.

Tucked in a corner of his desk was a small book, *The Person Who Is Down*, which had been given to him when he was a young man.[18] Many mornings he would hold it in his hands for a few moments, not reading it, just remembering what its message meant to him.

When I slept overnight at my grandparents' house I would get out of bed early to go into the den, still in my pajamas, and sit with my grandfather. One day I asked him why he would so often pick up that one little book.

"Inside this book," he answered, "is a short talk that was given as encouragement for, as the title says, a person who is down. A long time ago it got me thinking about what really matters. Most people experience many times when they feel down. It's only natural because life is hard. That's why I take a moment to hold this little book. It reminds me that good things don't come from giving in to difficulties and wearing them around like a weight on our shoulders. Instead, we have to toughen up so we can give our best to life."

Even though my grandfather's days were difficult the whole time I knew him, right up to the day he died when I was sixteen, it didn't stop him from trying to learn and grow, or from trying to help me find my way in the world. Despite his impairments, he was one of the strongest men I have ever known. His handshake was like iron and his hugs squeezed the wind out of me.

"What do you mean by 'toughen up'?" I asked him that morning. "Work harder?"

"No," he said, "work differently, see things differently. The best people I have known were tough enough to stay focused on what they really cared about. They said 'no' to the rest. And they came through, for their family, friends, and organization, even when things were rough."

I thought about that. "It sounds like they were heroes," I said.

"No, in more ways than I ever realized years ago, they were just like you and me," my grandfather said. "Ordinary people. Most were quiet about what they did and avoided the limelight. What set them apart, it seems to me, was how tough and calm and inventive they were, all at the same time. They came at challenges in their own best way, differently than most people do. These men and women are the ones I remember each morning."

I have found that, like these rare individuals, you and I can prepare ourselves to be mentally, physically, and emotionally resilient in the face of adversity. We can learn to toughen up and grow more as a result of life's harshest tests.[19] When you do that, research shows you'll be healthier, too.[20]

But here's the key: You must build toughness *before* you need it—one choice at a time, one action at a time.

Recall Your Best Whenever You Need It

Toughness begins by preparing yourself in advance to elicit surges of your best mental or physical energy whenever you need them. One of the simplest and most effective techniques for doing this is *anchoring*.[21]

In some ways, holding *The Person Who Is Down* in his hands was an anchor for my grandfather. Anchoring happens throughout our lives, in both good and bad ways. For example, consider the waves of memory that hit you when you hear a special song, even many years after you last heard it. That song is an anchor. Or recall the strong feelings you immediately get from vividly recalling any of your great moments—or worst moments—in sports, art, school, public speaking, when interacting with others, at work, as a parent, or while traveling.

Subconscious negative or positive responses are associated with a variety of places and things in our lives. If you don't control negative images, they can flood the mind and hit you with waves of anxiety. That anxiety can be particularly crippling in times of pressure and change.

Much of how we see ourselves and the world around us is primarily a choice we make. Anchors allow you to choose positive reinforcements of your best self instead of negative ones, and to instantly recall those positive images whenever you need them.[22]

Here's how to create an anchor of your best self—the self you want to bring to situations that are difficult or daunting.

Sit in a comfortable, quiet place and take some time to relax deeply. Then vividly imagine yourself thinking, feeling, looking, sounding, and performing with excellence in a specific past circumstance. Real-life experiences are best, but imaginary circumstances can also be effective. View the mental picture in slow motion. Summon an image of yourself at your best: a time when you were able to respond effortlessly, no matter how demanding or intricate the challenge. Recall your finest moment in every detail, using every sense—touch, sound, sight, along with your intuition and feelings. Your goal is to etch that memory into your consciousness so that you can summon it in an instant when facing a challenge.

At the peak moment of the remembered or imagined experience, make a unique sensory signal to yourself. For example, you might choose any or all of the following: a *touch* (such as your thumb against the second knuckle of your index finger with a specific amount of pressure), a *mental picture* (of yourself in a fluid state of confidence and control, performing at your best), or a *silent, personally meaningful word or phrase* (such as "calm," "confident," "clear mind," "excel," "let's go," "creative," or "I *can* handle this.").

Wait half an hour or so and then repeat the process. Later that day, test your anchor. Re-create the quiet, relaxed scene. Then, as you imagine starting your day tomorrow or responding to the first sign of a stressful situation in which you'd like to recapture your sense of the "best moment" state, initiate your anchor by "firing" the sensory signals—in this example we used touch, a mental picture, and a silent word or phrase.

Head First

You can eventually create a number of anchors to replace unproductive thoughts and feelings with positive ones. You can also prepare yourself to make the best of challenging times by learning to manage negative thoughts as they arise, rather than correcting later for their corrosive effects. As Eleanor Roosevelt said, "You gain courage and confidence by strengthening your mind, one challenge after another."[23]

To begin with, understand this unhappy paradox: If you allow your mind to focus on preventing a bad outcome instead of bringing about a good one, your brain can get entrapped by the negative, making the bad outcome even more likely to occur.[24] Negative suggestion works, bringing about in reality the worries and other victimizing traits that are imagined. By habit, we can be masters at unintentionally making ourselves unhappy.

Many of us have years of practice with put-downs, whether on the giving or receiving end. According to one estimate, the national average of parent-to-child criticisms is 12 to 1—a dozen criticisms for every single compliment or positive word. In the average secondary school classroom, the ratio of criticisms to compliments from teacher to student is 18 to 1.[25] Researchers have reported that in business situations the average negative-to-positive ratio ranges from 4 to 1 to 8 to 1.[26]

Knowing which thoughts to emphasize and which to let go of helps you toughen up in advance of any difficulties you will face. You can prepare yourself to use negative thoughts as a trigger for positive responses, acting immediately to do something productive instead of destructive. Eventually, you can identify the sources of most negative thoughts and remove them. Negative thoughts caused by tension or anxiety tend to get bigger if you give in to them, but they can be relieved by the strategic pauses and physical exercises described later in this chapter, and controlled by the Instant Calming Sequence detailed in Chapter 2.

For now, recognize that you do not have to do the impossible and banish all negative thoughts from your mind. Instead, you can turn negatives into positives by applying what is called "defensive pessimism."

Defensive pessimists grow from adversity by first assuming worst-case challenges for upcoming events or circumstances, and then reviewing a wide range of options for preventing or responding to them.[27] They spend time mentally rehearsing various approaches and responses to problems until there is a strong sense of confidence in having the best chance of succeeding. They *anticipate* the possibility of disappointment or failure, but then they apply themselves to making things turn out better.

What makes defensive pessimism a valuable tool for some people in building mental toughness is that it produces hope and focuses on facing up to anxiety-producing situations and working through them, rather than avoiding them or giving in to them.

So if you're a natural optimist, fine. But if you're not, stop listening to people who tell you that all you have to do is look on the bright side. Go ahead and look on the gloomy side, and then use defensive pessimism to excelerate toward positive outcomes.

Shouldering the Hard Things

Here's one of the simplest and most effective ways I have found to build more of the inner toughness it takes to face and overcome challenges. Regularly ask yourself the following two questions:

1. *What's the most difficult thing you've done this week?*
2. *What's the most difficult thing you will do next week?*

Jot these questions on an index card and post it nearby. Schedule a regular time each week to think about your response. Keep a running account of your answers on a note pad or in a daybook. Use this process to challenge the edges of your comfort zone. Each time you recognize that you've made progress—no matter how small—in facing a difficult situation, or are preparing to step forward to shoulder something more difficult next week, you toughen up a bit more.

As you take a moment to reflect on your answer, ask: Was this the best you could give? Is there any way you could have given something more or deeper or better?

On a weekly basis—Friday is my favorite day for doing this—you might ask the same question of others, those who work with you, or loved ones, or friends. Listen to each other's answers. It can change the way you think about yourself and other people, and it can help you discern new ways to make a greater difference.

That's another thing this simple mechanism does: it provides a direct and unexpected way to value the seemingly minor, yet often profound acts of daring or commitment all around us that few of us would otherwise know about. Day after day, every one of us is capable of small, yet exceptional acts of initiative and caring, despite the fact that most of them may be unnoticed by others. It's worth the effort. Research shows that small, positive behaviors are a primary driver of lasting positive attitudes, not the other way around.[28]

This small exercise encourages you to do more hard things, and take more smart risks. Practice stepping forward to do them without resentment or complaint, as acts of character or to stretch your capabilities. When you vary the kinds of hard things you do, it also helps you make peace with being uncomfortable. And that keeps you growing and toughening up.

A distinctive, learning-filled life results from a succession of small, specific choices made each day. There's a world of difference between imagining such a fulfilling life and actually living it. It is through taking new actions that we learn to awaken and apply our hidden capacities.[29]

Well Begun Is Half Done

My grandfather taught me that it's easy to let the day run you, instead of you running the day, and it all begins first thing in the morning. Research has proven him right. So, whenever possible, start your morning with a power-on routine that gives you extra energy to withstand stress and better handle challenges all day.

Here it's important to know that there are two primary kinds of energy. Researchers contrast them by calling one *tense energy* and the other *calm energy*.[30] Most of us are entrapped by tense energy, a stress-driven state characterized by a nearly constant sense of pressure and anxiety.

Fueled by emergency stress hormones such as adrenaline and cortisol, tense energy keeps you going because it engages your limbic system and reticular activating system, key brain areas that respond to any whiff of danger by kicking your energies into high gear. You can either stand and fight or run away—as fast as possible. Although they are magnificently adapted for survival, those brain areas contain not an ounce of creativity, vision, or thoughtful reflection. All they can cause you to do is more of what you've always done—only faster, harder, longer, and louder.

You may awaken tired and stiff in the morning, but after several cups of coffee and some heavy tension—worrying about all the work you have to do, sweating over the latest news from the stock markets, cursing in rush-hour traffic—you may soon feel "energized." That kind of energy compels you to push yourself toward one objective after another without pausing to rest or reflect. Minor irritations and small stumbles loom up as major frustrations. Errors keep cropping up: research shows that people who are in a hurry make 20 to 25 percent more mistakes than they do when they are working normally.[31] As a result of all those factors, your efforts become infused with a moderate to severe level of physical tension, which may eventually become only barely perceptible to you.

But that psychological and physical "energy" is costly: underneath the stress-hormone-induced buzz, the billions of messenger chemicals that connect your senses and heart with your brain are being depleted. By the end of a typical tense-energy day they may be all but gone, leaving you with only the stamina required to collapse mindlessly in front of the television or the computer.

Calm energy, on the other hand, stills the ancient brain's overreaction tendencies and accesses many of your highest capabilities. The calm energy state is characterized by low muscle tension, an alert presence of mind, peaceful body feelings, increased creative intelligence, physical vitality, and a deep sense of well-being.

With calm energy, you make far more progress throughout the day because you can focus more clearly on the things that are important to you without becoming consumed by needless divergences or inessential details. You have the mental and physical equivalent of an overdrive gear in a car, still moving quickly, but with far less strain.

When you develop the ability to enter and maintain a state of calm energy, you more effectively distance yourself from life's noise and distractions, its rushing and anger. You promote increased clearmindedness and sustained vitality. You discover more ingenuity—even moments of fun—in the face of skyrocketing pressure, constant uncertainty, and continued change.

With a few simple adjustments in the way you manage your day, you can stop the gear-grinding effects of tense energy and shift into calm energy, beginning first thing in the morning.

Here's how:

- ***Start the day right.*** Lots of people set their alarms as late as possible and then leap out of bed in a last-minute rush to begin the day. The result is a tension-producing shock to the system. Blood pressure soars as stress hormones pour into the bloodstream. Instead, step—don't leap—out of bed, giving your muscles a chance to ease into action.

In the first few minutes after awakening, think of the things you can look forward to—areas of promise and excitement, instead of just more drudgery and worry. Imagine yourself at your best. Remember the instant power of anchoring—having fun and getting many of the right things accomplished, with a lot less strain than before. This initial impression of what's ahead really matters to your energy level. Your creativity is also waiting for these signals.

- ***Absorb some light.*** The brain responds to many signals, but few are more powerful than light. There is a neurological link between the retina of the eye and the suprachiasmatic nuclei in your brain, which play an important role in your ability to focus your attention and energy production.[32] In most cases, the more light, the more focus and calm energy.

Progressively turn on twice the number of lights you'd usually turn on. Leave those lights on for the first 10 or 15 minutes that you're awake. Or step outside for a minute or so to flood your eyes with daylight. Feel the difference in energy.

- ***Move into the day.*** Get at least five minutes of light physical activity each morning. There are lots of options here: a walk, slowly climbing and descending a few flights of stairs, or pedaling at a relaxed, moderate pace on a stationary bike or outdoor cycle. For variety you might do some moderate muscle-toning exercises. Any of those activities send a signal to the brain to toughen up and increase calm energy.

- *Eat smart.* Now it's time to eat a few bites of the meal that matters most, the meal that half of all Americans still skip. When you eat a small serving of a healthy breakfast you switch on, and turn up, your vitality. So try a bowl of oatmeal with low-fat or skim milk and a piece of fruit, or a slice of whole-grain bread with nonfat cream cheese and all-fruit preserves or a small serving of salmon. When this food reaches the stomach it triggers responses in the brain and senses that are essential to mind-body toughness and calm energy through the morning and into the afternoon.

Keep Pulling Back to Get Ahead

The Achilles heel in our nonstop world isn't that we lack urgency or willpower to drive us, it's that we lack sufficient alertness and preparation to rely on calm energy instead.[33]

To pay exceptional attention to your life and work, you must have the motivation, of course, but it's just as important to turn on the brain's alertness switches. "A person's alertness is triggered by key internal and external factors that can be considered the switches on the control panel of the mind," says Dr. Martin Moore-Ede, one of the preeminent researchers examining the biology of star performance. "Understanding these key switches and how to manipulate them is the secret of gaining power over one of the most important attributes of the human brain."[34]

Alertness leads to the right kind of attentiveness, where you pay attention to what really matters and exclude what doesn't, freeing your energy to fluidly interact with your priorities. In this state, which is essential to excelerating, the brain and senses hum and purr, and ingenious ideas for solving old problems and new dilemmas drop into the mind with ease.

A simple, yet very powerful, way to turn on your brain's alertness switches is to introduce short breaks throughout the day.[35]

I call these short breaks *strategic pauses*, and they require just a minute or less every half-hour or so during the day. I have written about them at length in my recent book, *The Other 90%*; here I will summarize the key steps in sufficient detail for you to make this tool work for you right away. Here are the five quick steps to a strategic pause. Take one every half-hour.

1. Breathe. How well you breathe has a lot to do with how much energy and attentiveness you can generate and sustain all day long. Oxygen interruption—frequent brief halts in breathing, or chronic underbreathing—is a common contributing factor to tension and tiredness. Conversely, every time you deepen your breathing, you increase calmness and alertness. Take a moment right now to breathe in and let the air expand your lungs more than usual. Do you notice your posture lifting slightly or your senses sharpening? Breathe out fully and then take another lung-expanding breath. That's the idea.

2. Catch some light. Step to a window or glance at a bright indoor light. Change your view. Many people report a lasting sense of calmness followed by a surge of energy after looking at a bright outdoor scene or glancing at indoor light, even at the intensity level of normal room lamps.

3. Loosen up and stand taller. Begin by standing up—tall, loose, and at ease. For those of us who spend long periods of the day sitting down, there is evidence that simply standing up every half hour or so increases alertness and energy. Poor posture—even a slight slumping of the shoulders—depletes lung capacity by as much as 30 percent.[36] Keep your chin slightly in, head high, muscles relaxed, and you will significantly increase oxygen flow to your brain and senses.

4. Sip ice water. One of the most overlooked reasons for lack of energy is lack of water. Water provides the medium for nerve impulse conduction, for the transmission of other biochemical processes, and for the muscle contractions that stimulate metabolism and generate energy. Even a slight dehydration—not enough to make you thirsty—can measurably deplete toughness and calm energy. By sipping extra water, you not only improve your overall health and resistance to illness, but also provide a repeated signal to your metabolism to keep your energy and attentiveness levels higher. This effect may be even more pronounced when the water is ice-cold—because when it reaches the stomach it stimulates increased energy production and raises alertness in the brain and senses.

5. Snack for sustained energy. Whenever you skip between-meal snacks, blood sugar falls and you are likely to experience increased fatigue and tension. Eating small nutritious meals, and snacks at mid-morning and mid-afternoon, help stabilize blood-sugar levels, which in turn optimize learning and performance.

People experiencing high levels of stress tend to eat less than usual. But as pressure subsides to a more constant, but still high level, many people begin to eat more than usual. The best way to prevent excess food intake while you're under stress is to exercise more and find other non-food outlets for tensions.

You might also explore the effect of spicy foods on your energy level. Try adding a dab of mustard or a dash of chili powder or hot sauce. Those spices may help increase your after-meal metabolic rate, according to some medical studies.[37] You may find that the hot spices help you sustain calm energy and make you less likely to stuff yourself because the flavor's so intense.

Whatever specific steps you choose to include in your daily performance routines, strategic pauses remind us of some larger principles. To get ahead, you have to be able to pull back. To be more fully present, you have to be able to withdraw. And to accomplish more, you sometimes have to do less, and do things differently, by taking more of the right breaks.

Get a Better Grip on Life

Every time I visited my grandfather's house, there was some kind of chore with my name on it. One of the jobs I liked least was straightening bent nails. But my grandfather was adamant—we never wasted anything. So I would collect bent nails whenever we built or repaired anything, and then he would lay them out on the workbench, all sizes of nails, from eight penny to sixteen penny, and even big pole barn nails. I would have to pound them straight again and put them in old paint cans that were stacked on shelves along the wall.

I remember the times when we were together in that garage and my grandfather would lean on his cane with one hand while with the other hand he lifted a paint can filled with nails. First with one arm and then with the other. Next, holding the handle with a few fingers. Then with one finger after another.

He made it look easy, even with the full cans, and he would say to me, "It's a good kind of exercise. It's how I get a better grip on life. If I keep my hands strong, it seems to help my mind be stronger, too." I've thought about that many times in the years that have followed, and research now confirms—as was so often true of my grandfather's intuitive perceptions—that there is truth to it. A large part of the brain is devoted to sensory and motor connections with the fingers. Enhanced brain function can come from improving the strength and dexterity of the fingers and hands.[38] Besides that, every way you build muscle tone in your hands and forearms also increases your overall energy level. Each toned muscle cell is like a little energy-producing furnace that helps burn off excess body fat twenty-four hours a day, even when you're sleeping.[39]

So, as part of your toughening-up regimen, *develop the hands of an artist or a rock climber.* Doing that is easier than you think, and you don't need an old paint can filled with nails. Grip a squeezable ball. Crumble scrap paper with one hand before tossing it into the recycling pile. Open and close your hands, slowly, using all the muscles you can feel in them.

Of course, for a better grip on life there are other parts of your physical self that need toughening, too. Such as:

• ***Build the heart of a lion.*** The heart is more than just a pump. Scientists can measure its radiating energy from more than five feet away.[40] It activates our deepest values, transforming them from things we just think about, to what we truly live. In a very practical way, the heart is the place of courage and spirit, integrity and commitment.

You build your physical heart by exercise—by regular walks or other forms of aerobic fitness. But you also build your true heart by your involvement with difficult situations—your own and those of others you care about, especially those who are less fortunate, including children and the elderly. Think about your life. How can you develop more heart—one day, one challenge, at a time?

• ***Develop the skin of a rhino.*** Albert Schweitzer left a comfortable life as a university professor, musician, and parish minister to go to medical school. Upon completing his studies, at age thirty-eight, he traveled to French Equatorial Africa, where he cleared the forest and built a hospital with his bare hands and his exceptional ingenuity. Then, for over fifty years, he served people with leprosy and sleeping sickness, and many others who would otherwise have suffered terribly from preventable illnesses or died long before their time.

Those who worked beside him in his hospital in Lambaréné, Africa, saw him struggle to provide care under extremely difficult conditions. It earned him the Nobel Peace Prize. His credo called for both courage and sensitivity of the highest order, and through the years, his work touched many people.

Once he was asked, "What does it take to create a life worth leading?" Schweitzer answered, "The skin of a rhino and soul of an angel."[41] As part of toughening up, it's important to develop a thick enough skin to meet the barbs and arrows of life while having the courage to say what you mean and mean what you say, even when others don't like it.

There are lots of small ways to practice this in daily life. Look around you. Notice how many people are critical of others or cynical about life's possibilities. If you listen to all of those comments and try to interpret all the body language other people convey, it's easy to end up feeling like you're being endlessly judged and rarely ever measure up. A thick skin means you can hear such pronouncements without necessarily listening to them.

On the other hand, some people have lived or worked with you for long enough to have earned the right to give you feedback. Their comments should always be taken into consideration. But most other people have not earned the right for you to listen to their criticisms, so don't. Accept that someone is almost always going to be mad at you, or envious, or negative—that's human nature. It's important to remember that our differences are also what make life interesting.

In truth, what other people convey—in what they think, feel, say, and do—is almost never about you; instead, it's almost always about them. If you take things too personally, you're destined for needless suffering at the hands of those who believe they can feel good only when their words or actions make someone else feel bad.

So practice thickening your skin. Don't gossip about others. Imagine barbed words bouncing off you instead of digging into you. Whenever you can, keep moving forward in the direction of your dreams instead of waiting for approval from others or letting their doubts infect you. Keep holding to your own values and standing on your own two feet.

With few exceptions, the only criticism worth considering is that from a trusted source, someone who has earned the right to give it by working or living side-by-side with you and coming to know you deeply, truly, and well.[42] But the world is ablaze with verbal put-downs and backtalk. It's the background chatter in many settings of life and work. So, it's important to practice thickening your skin by not letting critical words or pointed gossip get under your skin or into your heart—because if you let that happen, then you're giving up a piece of your attention and energy that could be used instead for something that truly matters.

• ***Toughen up your lungs and legs.*** Making it through tough times requires stamina. Without it, your spirit is likely to flag. Start by toughening up your lungs and legs. Regular aerobic exercise—such as walking, jogging, cycling, swimming, skating, and rowing—strengthens your ability to recover rapidly from high-stress situations.[43] It also enables you to respond more energetically and appropriately to challenges.[44]

Aerobic exercise is steady, rhythmic physical activity that increases your ability to deliver maximum amounts of oxygenated blood throughout the body and brain. A brisk walk is a good example. Aerobic exercise stimulates an optimal amount of the hormone norepinephrine.[45] Low norepinephrine levels are associated with feelings of helplessness and a low tolerance for adversity.[46] Physical exercise is also beneficial to the limbic system,[47] which has a number of receptors to receive the mood-boosting endorphins produced during exercise. When the natural amino acid tryptophan enters your brain, it enhances your energy and toughness—and also helps burn off excess stress hormones.

Before beginning any fitness program, check with your physician regarding your readiness. Once you're involved with a regular aerobics routine, consider adding some variety—and further boosting your resilience—with easy speed-ups and slow-downs. Once you can exercise at a comfortable, moderate pace, add some intervals where you change the pace to go faster, then slower. The goal is to develop increased recovery ability.[48]

Be sure to follow your body's signals—you should never feel pain when exercising.

• ***Develop the stomach for challenges.*** The core of all strength in the body is in the abdominal muscles.[49] From them comes the ability to exert and resist force. A weak abdominal area can be linked to lower back pain and problems with posture, movement, and breathing.[50]

Two specific muscles, the transversalis and the pyramidalis, strengthen your lower abdomen and protect your lower back.[51] Those muscles can be toned by a simple breathing exercise I call the *transpyramid*. Sit or stand in an upright, comfortable position. Take a normal breath in, breathe out, and then forcibly blow out as much air from your lungs as you can, allowing your *lower* abdomen (which is where these two key muscles are located) to come in and up as much as possible. At first, you might use your hands to gently push inward and upward on the lower abdomen during the exhalation part of the exercise.

Now try the exercise again. Slowly exhale and as you reach the place where you normally finish breathing out, smoothly and forcefully breathe out more, using the power of your *lower* abdominal muscles. Work up to doing a total of ten of these exercises each day.[52]

Next, strengthen the middle and upper abdomen with modified crunches or curl-ups. Lie on your back on a padded or carpeted surface, with your knees bent and your feet flat on the floor. Cross your arms on your chest or clasp your hands lightly behind your head. With your middle and lower back flat on the floor, slowly raise your head and shoulders slightly off the ground, not more than about 30 degrees. Keep your lower abdomen flat; do not let your lower back arch or your stomach stick out during the upward movement. Pause for a second at the top of the motion and then slowly lower yourself to the original position. Begin with only a few repetitions and, as long as there is no serious discomfort or pain, over a period of weeks work your way up to 25 or more repetitions every other day.

• *Know when to turn off the "on" button.* As noted previously, tension is a primary saboteur of excelerating. Calm effectiveness depends on knowing how to turn off your "on" button, and then doing it. Sometimes, it's a physical slowdown that's needed. Some of us are really good at staying very, very busy, which can be bad, especially because not all motion is useful and not all movement is forward, or, as my mother used to say, "The hurrier you go, the nuttier you get." If you find yourself in this place, step off the fast track and relax your body for at least a few minutes. Hard, isn't it? You have to be tough to resist rushing and know when and how to relax well.

But what if it's your mind that never seems to stop racing, even when your body's at ease? If that's the case, start trying ways to send your mind on a brief holiday, even in the middle of the day. There are many benefits from finding this disengage switch. As research shows, creative intelligence significantly increases when you stop rushing and think *less*, not more.[53]

In certain islands of the Caribbean, this is known as *liming*—the art of doing nothing, or anything healthy that you enjoy doing, guilt-free.[54] Sometimes the only way to get ahead is to step back, at least for a little while, and that's the power of liming time.

In short, to toughen up and excelerate, you have to get really good at letting go.

• ***Rest well to renew your inner reserves.*** Whenever you're under stress, rest takes on special importance. Resilience requires superb recovery, and that means deep sleep. When you toss and turn all night, you steadily lose your hardiness and calm energy.

To sleep more deeply tonight, get up after your evening meal and go for a light walk for at least five minutes. Doing so will give you up to twice your usual evening energy, and also deepen your sleep by raising your body's core temperature within three to five hours before you fall asleep.[55] Hide your clock, so you don't keep partially awakening through the night to look at it, and make the bedroom as dark as possible, since even small amounts of light can disturb deep rest.[56]

As you drift into sleep, relax your body. Reestablish your perspective. Appreciate your blessings. Think inspiring thoughts. These things matter. "Even a soul submerged in sleep is hard at work," said Heraclitus, "and helps make something of the world."

2

Calm Down
...to respond with poised effectiveness to pressure and uncertainty.

You do not simply exist, but always decide what your life will be, and what you will become in the next moment.
—Viktor Frankel

Calmness under pressure isn't something we're born with, and attitude or willpower won't produce it, yet it is learnable at any age.[57]

This chapter presents a new view of one of the simplest yet most effective ways to build calm effectiveness to speed through challenges. This compliments the message of the proceeding chapter: the ability to handle life's biggest challenges is developed through learning to master small situations of pressure and difficulty.[58] How you handle everyday friction spots—delays, interruptions, disappointments, hurt feelings, financial worries, traffic jams, and deadlines, to name just a few—is an important predictor of your effectiveness in meeting large challenges and bouncing back from setbacks. It's also an indicator of your overall psychological and physical health.[59]

When you stay calm under pressure, you can use your inner resources more wisely, instead of letting the brain's ancient instincts trigger waves of tension or fear. Negative emotions can seriously interfere with work and life, diverting energy and attention from the challenge or task before you.[60] Stress hormones from such negative feelings continue to circulate through the bloodstream, many hours after the incident that caused them, has ended.[61] Research also shows that when you let stressful events become distressing, it erodes your thinking abilities and thwarts crucial social skills, such as empathy.[62]

Take Charge of Stressful Moments with the Instant Calming Sequence

The key skill for calming down begins with noticing every one of the pressure-packed little turning points during your day, and responding to them in simple, effective ways at the instant they appear.[63]

At the very first moment you feel a flash of anger, surge of fear, or any kind of increased negative stress, you can trigger what I call the *Instant Calming Sequence* (ICS). Because it is performed while you are fully alert, with eyes open, the ICS may be used unobtrusively in a wide range of circumstances.

Without the ICS, the tension and emotion of a situation can "take you over." When that happens, you may lose control. People say, "I don't know what happened. It wasn't me. It's like I became a different person." You did. The situation ran you, not the other way around. Chemical and hormonal changes in the brain and body can do that to you, instantly tensing you up and unleashing negative emotions that make it very difficult— often just plain impossible—to reverse your first, counterproductive reactions.

With practice, you will find yourself applying the ICS without conscious thought, using the new brain pathways you have developed.

The Instant Calming Sequence (ICS)

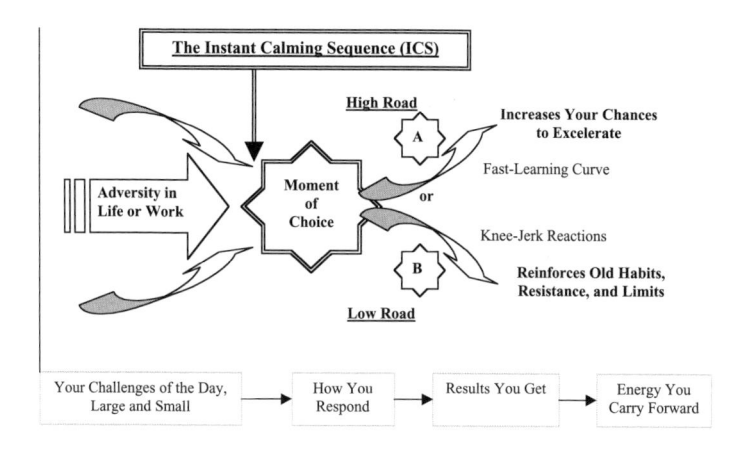

Adversity in Life or Work → Moment of Choice

- **High Road (A)**: Increases Your Chances to Excelerate — Fast-Learning Curve
- **Low Road (B)**: Knee-Jerk Reactions — Reinforces Old Habits, Resistance, and Limits

Your Challenges of the Day, Large and Small → How You Respond → Results You Get → Energy You Carry Forward

When you use the ICS to insert calm alertness at the very start of each stressful or fearful scene, you create a "gap in the action" between a stimulus and response. Over time you learn to enlarge that gap to accomplish many important things, such as using your creative imagination to seek out new solutions; focusing on what you *can* control rather than what you can't; stopping your mind from knotting you up in imaginary fears; listening for a moment longer with an open mind instead of blindly talking back; or seeing how you can protect yourself without harming others.

The five steps of the Instant Calming Sequence (ICS) are:

1. Continue breathing
2. Lighten your eyes
3. Uplift your posture
4. Acknowledge reality
5. Mobilize your best

I encourage you to put this idea to the test. I will describe each step briefly, and then show how they are put into practice.

- *Step 1: Continue Breathing.* When we are tense or anxious, our breathing tends to become shallow and intermittent. Because oxygen is vital to life, the body and brain are extremely sensitive to even very small reductions in its availability.[64] Moreover, the ease and rhythm of your breathing must also serve as a natural stimulus to the inner breathing of the hundred trillion cells in your body that enable you to produce biological energy, and in particular calm energy. If you unknowingly halt your breathing during the first moments of a stressful situation, as many people do, it propels you toward feelings of anxiety, panic, anger,
frustration, and a general loss of control.[65]

So, notice when pressures rise, and consciously keep you breathing going without interruption. Keep it smooth and steady.

- *Step 2: Lighten Your Eyes.* The muscles of the face not only react to our mood, they help set it. When your face or jaw (or both) are tense, within moments that tension spreads throughout the body and affects your thinking. Easing off on the intensity in your eyes and, at the same time, maintaining a neutral facial expression—or, even better, a slightly positive one—can make a big difference during stressful situations.[66]

Try this the next chance you get. One reason for the quickness and power of this response is that positive reactions in the facial muscles increase blood flow to the brain and transmit nerve impulses from the face and eyes to the limbic system, where your immediate reactions are guided. Lightening the eyes and smiling even slightly changes neurochemistry toward favorable emotions and more constructive actions.

- **Step 3: Uplift Your Posture.** Rigid posture increases closed-mindedness and perhaps makes it more likely that you will be victimized.[67] Therefore, it's vital to make certain your position is unlocked—relaxed, upright, neutral, and tall.

Test this yourself right now by assuming a tight, slumped posture, perhaps in front of a full-length mirror. Say something. Does it feel natural? Does it feel strained, weak, or grouchy? Now choose to unlock your position, both mentally and physically, with a balanced neutral stance and open peaceful hands. Begin talking again. Do you notice the difference? Whenever you react to stressful situations with a slouching posture you magnify feelings of helplessness and panic.[68]

Unlocking your position is one of the surest ways to overcome a common, debilitating reaction to fear or danger known as *somatic retraction*. This is a slouching posture characterized by tightening or collapsing the chest, rolling the shoulders forward and down, and tensing the abdomen, back, or neck. Merely thinking of a threatening situation can make you automatically tense up.

Certain areas of the body have large corresponding "maps" in the brain and can help you calm down more quickly and effectively. Two of those "signal muscle areas" are the face and hands. One way to unlock your position is to flash a mental "wave of relaxation" through your whole body, beginning with the muscles in your face and around your eyes and then right out through your fingertips and toes—as if you're standing tall under a waterfall that clears away all excess tension.

- **Step 4: Acknowledge Reality.** This ICS step takes molehills masquerading as mountains and turns them back into molehills. Far too many of us get tangled up bemoaning every challenge we face. "Not *another* problem! Why does this *always* happen to me?"

By wishing the situation weren't happening, regretting that you didn't have more time to prepare, wishing you were somewhere else, or anguishing over life's unfairness, you set off a biochemical wildfire of victimizing thoughts and feelings. You actually help yourself lose control and become loaded up with anxiety and frustration. A single mishandled moment of stress can disrupt an entire day. The ICS breaks that pattern.

Another one of the fastest ways to get trapped in old negative patterns is to instantly identify a new challenge or problem as if it were just like—or similar to, but even worse than—a previous stressful event. Example: "*Not again!*" you think. Or, "He's *always* doing that!" In this ICS step, you *notice uniqueness*. You take a moment of awareness to identify the unique features of this situation or challenge, pinpointing some of the ways it's different from anything you've dealt with before.

For example, if someone you live with has a tendency to come in the door exhausted and angry at day's end, and you feel yourself getting upset. Instead of assuming today's pressures are just the same as every other day for this loved one, pause for a split second to empathize. Wonder, or ask, what might have been different about today's work and commute. Perhaps this day's tension is based on wanting to be home—instead of stuck in traffic—because it's Friday, or it's someone's birthday, or it's time for some much-needed fun with the family in a crazy world.

By doing that, you bypass the brain's innate, lightning-fast tendency to magnify negative presumptions about people and situations, and instead you have a good chance of strengthening your relationship instead of inadvertently breaking it down.[69]

• ***Step 5: Mobilize Your Best.*** In virtually every challenge there is a hidden opportunity to practice what we value—and to learn something new—if we mobilize our best.

Here is where you might apply an anchor—the split-second way of inserting a precise and powerful image of excelling that I described in Chapter 1—so you can take the high road instead of the low road. The key thought is this: "What's happening is real and I'm calling upon the best in myself right now" or "Am I about to be the best person I can be?"

Sometimes a dangerous or life-changing situation demands that you leap into action immediately, and the ICS prepares you to do this. But, in many cases it's wise *not* to take action right away. More often than most people realize, mobilizing your best may mean finding a way to buy some extra time—perhaps to learn more about the challenge you're facing. Or to advance gradually instead of rushing headlong into things. That's the power of the ICS: it lets you choose how, and exactly when, you respond to a challenging situation, instead of letting the situation run you.

The four aspects of excelerating presented in the chapters that follow will help you apply your best self, once the ICS and the other methods in this chapter have eased you past the initial confrontation with uncertainty, adversity, or challenge.

Identify Your Hot Buttons—and Respond with the ICS

There are many everyday opportunities to rehearse using the ICS. For example, think of the many "minor" frustrations that can arise at work and at home. "What do you mean you forgot to tell me?" "Why didn't you call to say you'd be late?" "Who left these clothes by the door?" "No one noticed the work I did!" "What was all that yelling while I was trying to talk on the phone?" "There's no place to park!" "Who left the lights on?" or "Why didn't someone else notice that the dog needed to go outside?"

In every life and workplace, there are an untold number of

these little hot buttons. Even if we could force ourselves not to talk about them or to pretend we don't notice them, they can still grow into something daunting and debilitating if they're not attended to. I'm reminded of the joke about the spiritual retreat center whose residents took a vow of silence, which could only be broken once a month by one selected person. The first month, the chosen person stood up at the appointed time and said, "The mashed potatoes are always cold." A month passed, and the next person stood up when it was his turn and said, "Lumpy, too." After another month, the third person said, "I'm leaving. I can't stand this constant bickering."

Devoting some brief time to identifying and addressing the hot buttons in yourself and the people around you will go far toward freeing up the energy and focus required to discover and develop more of your capabilities.

The ICS is designed to overcome habits that have become ingrained and automatic. Therefore, it's vital to bring your typical reactions into focus if you want to change them.[70] Create a simple chart like the one below in a notebook or daybook:

Hot Buttons → Calming Strategy (ICS) → Desired Outcomes

_____   _____   _____

In the left-hand column, list five or six of the small frustrations that knock you off balance. Then circle the three that affect you most strongly. Use that trio as your training ground for applying the ICS. Across from each of them, write a specific desired outcome.

For example:

Hot Buttons ➔ Calming Strategy (ICS) ➔ Desired Outcomes

Traffic jam	ICS	Use time to relax, remember what matters, think about creative ideas.

The ICS provides the bridge from the frustration to the desired outcome. First, imagine the stressful situation or moment of adversity. Vividly imagine—in extra-slow motion—that this particular tension-producing or pressure-filled situation is just beginning to happen. Stall the stress signal right there. Now picture yourself effortlessly, successfully going through the ICS: (1) continue breathing, (2) lighten your eyes, (3) unlock your position, (4) notice uniqueness, and (5) acknowledge reality and mobilize your best.

Remember, the ICS is a natural, flowing sequence. You release it; you don't force it. Practice it a number of times a day, using different stress cues, increasing the vividness of the mental images and the speed of your ICS response. If at first you have difficulty with any of the steps, practice them one at a time until you feel comfortable with them. If you get partway into the ICS and feel yourself starting to lose control, back the sequence up and slow things down.

You are training to automatically slip the ICS into a situation right behind the first signal of stress or tension. When rehearsing for especially intense situations, you might try lightening the image of the pressure cue (by seeing yourself move farther away from it in your mind, or by dulling the vividness of the scene) until you are at ease with using the ICS to handle it.

Keep Assessing Your Progress—
So You Can Make More of It

Following each response to a challenging situation, ask yourself: Have I just acted like the person I want to be? Did I remain cool and focused, responding based on my values and true priorities? If things fell apart, what was the moment when that breakdown began? How could I catch it earlier and better next time?

Ask those around you: Was my response calmer and more effective this time? What could I improve? Listen and learn. Modify your practice accordingly.

By the way, be patient with yourself. The really tough challenges often require quite a bit of practice before you can smoothly excelerate through them. Remember that most of us have had years of training strengthening the counterproductive reactions that the ICS can replace. Fortunately, it's easier than you might have realized to keep building positive qualities into your life and work—and it's never too late to stop being limited by old habits.

3

See Near and *Far*

...to pay exceptional attention to what's right in front of you without losing sight of where you are trying to go.

Vision is the art of seeing things nearby and far away that are invisible to everyone else.

—Jonathan Swift

When I was in my early teenage years I learned to sail at a summer camp where I had a part-time job. One bright July day, on a calm lake, I was gaining confidence and my instructor, anxious to head off to give other lessons, said, "Okay, Robert, you're on your own."

He clambered into a passing canoe and headed back toward shore. There wasn't much wind. The small sailboat was maneuverable. I was wearing a lifejacket. I was pleased to learn that sailing wasn't so difficult after all.

Then a bank of black clouds rolled in without warning from the west and the wind picked up. The temperature dropped and a sharp rain soon followed, stinging my eyes. There were waves now, lots of them. The wind caught the sail and almost tipped the boat. I desperately tried to regain control, but realized I was being blown farther out into the lake.

I was struggling to see near and far at the same time. I needed to sense the direction to the shore while being intensely focused on the task at hand, trying to figure out how to keep the boat upright and turn it around.

Fortunately for me, the storm passed almost as quickly as it had come. I tacked my way numbly back to shore, relieved to be safe and finished with sailing for the day. But I have always remembered the feeling.

Unlike that day on the lake, some of life's storms don't stop very quickly, and we need to develop our skill at seeing both near and far to make our way safely through them.

During difficult situations, it's important to acknowledge that the world is unpredictable and sometimes very complicated. Because of this, you must position yourself to see and sense as much of it up-close as you can, while dealing with the essential tasks at hand. At the same time, you must maintain your distance vision and faith that your overall course will turn out to be a good one in the long run.

In short, you must learn to see near *and* far. If you only see far-off into the future, you may look right past what's in front of you and find that in the present moment you are sinking. On the other hand, if your time horizon is too short and you're wholly immersed in what's right in front of you, small things appear huge. You struggle with the sail, but lose your direction. Everything gets warped out of perspective.

We need to combine both viewpoints at once, but they are developed one at a time.

Observe More of What's Right in Front of You

Up close, that's where most of life must be lived.
—Epictetus

John Muir once wrote, "Most people live on the world, not in it." To excelerate is to live *in* the world, not just on it, and to do this you must become skilled at zeroing in on what's happening up close, right now. Here's one place to start:

• *Practice being a passionate observer—and notice what others miss.* My grandfather had a small book in his library called "The Passionate Observer," a translation of a work composed in 1879 by Jean Henri Fabré, the most famous entomologist of his era. It was about bugs. Fabré described a dragonfly's translucent wings in the brilliant sunlight of the French countryside, gleaming like small stained glass windows. He made a grasshopper seem as though it were made of gleaming jade against a muted branch.

When I walked with my grandfather in the fields, hilltops, and gardens near my grandparents' home, he would ask me to tell him what I observed in the miniature world beneath our footsteps, or in the grasses and brambles. Once I began to observe, I realized how much I had failed to notice before, always in some rush to finish work or go play. I have found that this is a worthy lesson for life.

Nearly all of the memorable, useful inventions of history have become reality because someone kept searching the richness of life's sights and saw what no one else had seen. It's remarkable how often we say things like, "It was right in front of my eyes, how could I have missed it?" "I should have thought of that." "I should have seen that."

The problem is that we keep looking with the same old expectations and preset limitations. So, one simple tool here is to practice seeing what no one else sees. Slow your breath and extend your senses. Look deeper. See more. The lost coin on the ground. The uniquely colored flower in the garden or alongside the path. The child's smile as you walk down a crowded grocery store aisle. The hidden image in the background of the picture. The shape of the clouds rolling overhead. A footprint in the sandy shore. A new seasoning or spice in a meal. A beautiful little colored shell on the beach. The person sitting alone at a child's birthday party. The elderly person struggling to open a door.

To see in this way, you have to suspend the quick closure that the brain tends to use on autopilot or in tunnel vision, and stay intensely curious a little longer. Sense deeper. Tune in. Look for something hidden. This enables you to respond in new ways.

Practice this skill when you walk into a room at home, work, or anywhere. What's different here? Ask yourself, "What's distinctive in what I see?" "How else could I look at this?" Surprise yourself. How much more of life's surprises and mysteries might you notice with just a little extra attention?

Here are several other small actions that are useful for sharpening up-close vision:

• *Put your current reality under the microscope.* Only by seeing more clearly where you are, can you actually change it into where you want to be.

Think about your to-do list today—and the things you've actually been doing from minute to minute and hour to hour since you got up this morning. Make a quick estimate of how much of your effort has been treading water, getting by, or merely hanging on. Only when you can look with crystal clarity at how you're living life *today*—and then link this forward into the future—can you make the changes that truly pay off over time.

• *Emphasize your sphere of influence, not your sphere of worries.* Within your *sphere of worries* is all the stuff you have no control over but which distracts you or leaves you feeling overwhelmed or incapacitated. That creates the worst kind of stress, because it's so completely purposeless.

It's important to note that, in some people, *brief* bouts of worry can actually be very constructive. I discussed this quality of "defensive pessimism" in Chapter 1. This kind of worry can be a positive driving force insofar as it centers your attention and efforts on your *sphere of influence*, which consists of all the things that your thoughts, feelings, and actions have a chance of shaping in some way, however small, for the better.

On a notepad, make two columns, one headed "Sphere of Worries" and the other headed "Sphere of Influence." List several things that fall into each of those categories for you.

Whenever you find yourself worrying about things you *can't* influence, even if you can't stop worrying, at least redirect your attention to something you *can* influence. Each time you do that, you shape your brain and senses to deal more constructively with the choices that are right in front of you.

• *Imagine your blessings.* To keep your bearings when immersing yourself in the up-close world, I've found that it really helps to keep in mind what you're most thankful for. Unless we make it a regular practice to remind ourselves of our blessings, it's easy for the brain's reticular activating system (discussed in the introductory chapter) to magnify the difficulties and negatives of our current situation, and leave us feeling at least a bit overwhelmed.

On a notepad or in a daybook, jot down some of your blessings. Think of all the things you have to be grateful for—the people and experiences that have meant the most to you through the years. Pick the top four and write them on an index card. Keep this card nearby and visible during the day. Pause at least once a day—mornings and evenings are my own favorite times for this—to not just *count* these blessings, as the old adage goes, but to briefly and vividly *imagine* them. By doing this you gather strength and inspiration that lasts not just for moments, but sometimes for hours.[71] This simple action can also stimulate the brain's visual cortex, which is involved not just in what we literally see around us but also in our intuition and anticipation of what's coming next.

See Far

Little Billy's mother was always telling him exactly what he was allowed to do and what he was not allowed to do. All the things he was allowed to do were boring. All the things he was not allowed to do were exciting. One of the things he was NEVER NEVER allowed to do, the most exciting of them all, was to go out beyond the gate all by himself and explore the world beyond.

—Roald Dahl

In *Dead Poets Society*, there's a scene when Robin Williams' character stops staring intently at a book in his hands, trying to understand it, and jumps up on a desk and looks around the room and then out the window into the distance. All at once, he has gained a new perspective and sees things clearly for the first time.

The idea in seeing far is to develop your own sensory radar that scans each situation and extends forward into the future—so you can clarify your bearings and assess your options for most effectively moving on. The future also helps put the present into better perspective for action. What may seem overwhelming today, can be accepted differently in the context of a bigger picture. It's usually only a rough patch on the long highway of life. When you think about it, it's pretty amazing how much influence something that doesn't even exist—the future—exerts on our understanding of what does exist: the present.

Look Farther Ahead Than You Have To

Before he retired, Ab Taylor was one of the U.S. Border Patrol's most renowned trackers. His extraordinary ability to see both near and far is a powerful metaphor for living our lives.

For forty years, in some of the most perilous conditions and daunting terrains, Ab was called in to find armed fugitives and lost youngsters. Always, his heart went out to the children. He was the one who would find these little ones whose cries for help had sometimes gone unheeded for many hours, or even days. These were children trapped in a nightmare. Some of them died. Others he found at the last moment and saved.

Watching Ab work evoked a sense of awe in me. He could sense the past and future, and draw them into the present to guide his steps. He could pick up a trail at any point and follow it, for hours or days if need be, through dense forest, day or night.

In the midst of confusing, contradictory, and disorganized information, he knew how to read every impression that can be made by a human being on the move. He knew what the weather and the passage of time did to tracks. In the still of the night or the roar of a storm he could follow old trails, including those all but obliterated beneath the footprints left by untrained searchers.

At the start, Ab would reach a point in the trail and swing his gaze from side to side, getting a quick, clear sense of the terrain—right here and far ahead. Then he would turn things over to his senses and begin tracking. To walk next to Ab Taylor when he was tracking was to witness a man moving quickly and gracefully, almost noiselessly, as he sensed the close-in and far-away signs. Ab knew he had not a single moment to spare.

What Ab Taylor faced was much like what many of us must deal with amid the pressures and uncertainties of our daily lives. We seek something just ahead, in the unknown, and we must marshal every asset at our disposal, every instinct, every kind of intelligence, to see us through. We can't afford to miss the signs ahead, or to drift far away from the track. The rational mind alone cannot accomplish all of this—we need at least a small degree of the abilities that Ab Taylor developed, so we can more effectively extend our awareness into the distance and future.

Here are several ways to increase that far-away vision:

• *Join a "tracker club."* Throughout the United States and around the world, there are scores of local clubs devoted to teaching intuitive awareness of natural conditions and sponsoring outdoor experiences where those skills are sharpened and put into practice. Even regular guided nature walks or bird-watching expeditions can help you create a kind of "sixth sense" that carries over into your everyday activities.[72]

• *Extend your senses 360°.* Stand up or lean forward in your chair and, no matter where you happen to be right now, imagine yourself being in the middle of a big room, filled with people and furniture, with large open windows.

Close your eyes and open your senses. Chances are, at first you will mostly notice what's very close by, such as the feel of this book in your hands or a person nearby or the ticking of a clock or the humming of a computer.

Now practice extending your senses. With your eyes closed, open your hands and extend your arms out in front of you, relaxed with elbows bent. Then bring them down to your sides.

How far away can you notice things? The breeze from an open window. The sound of a curtain moving. The squeak of someone's shoes. A furnace or air conditioner running far away. The footsteps or breathing of someone at the top of the stairway. The smell of food from the kitchen. The sound of a car engine outside, or a bird chirping. The whisper of a voice across the yard.

Now, while keeping your senses extended as far away as possible, open your eyes. I used to teach this simple exercise as a martial arts instructor during the time I served in the U.S. Marine Corps. It helps develop your skill at being more farseeing and calm in the middle of whatever challenges you face in the future.

- ***Survey the entire landscape, not just one corner of it.*** There are many different styles of perception in looking forward.[73] Some people have a natural tendency to imagine the best, others the worst, and some envision "impossible" things coming true. Excelerating depends on being able to blend all three. As you choose among possible directions to go forward, briefly glance ahead on each path and imagine the best-case scenario, and then the worst. Then try to guess which path has the best chance of positive surprises or hidden opportunities.

As you look ahead, remember to listen to your gut feelings.[74] Whenever we experience an emotion, it signifies that something personally important is happening. To anticipate what's next, heighten your ability to listen to your gut feelings and intuition. Instead of tuning in only to your thoughts, ask yourself, "What does my heart say about this?" "What is my gut instinct telling me?" The next time you face a challenge, as you get ready to choose your path forward, pause for an extra few moments to take all these sources of intelligence into account.

- ***Believing is seeing—so keep holding unshakable faith in the long view and big picture.*** According to researchers, those individuals who hold a clear distant vision are most likely to demonstrate leadership, thrive under pressure, earn higher incomes, and have happier and longer-lasting relationships.[75] But of course it's not just how far you can see, it's also *what* you see. Ask, "When I glance farther into the future, what do I want to create?"

In this sense, seeing isn't believing. That's backwards: Believing is seeing. Unless we expand our vision and curiosity, we see only what we expect to see, plan to see, or have the conditioning to notice. Everything else is unseen or just a blur, including the unexpected challenges that are sure to greet us as we move forward.

Now let's look at a simple, yet powerful tool for seeing near *and* far at the same time, and making it work in practical terms:

• ***Contrast where you are right now with what you want to become in five years.*** Who you want to become matters more than what you want to do or achieve. Research now shows that personal *development* goals lead to greater progress than do personal *performance* goals.[76] That is, when your aim is an achievement—for example, to win a trophy or make a certain amount of money or defeat an opponent—as an end in itself, you may merely be adding a new twist to doing what you usually do. Even if you win the prize, it likely won't result in much of an enduring advancement. On the other hand, when you focus on what you want to become in five years, that vision reveals areas of personal development that, if pursued, can transcend short-term gain for lasting progress.

Envision yourself and your life five years from today. What is your ideal picture of that future? What people would be close by? Where would you be when the sun rose or set? What would you need to be doing differently with your time and energy right now, and tomorrow and next month, if this were five years from now? This brief kind of envisioning is a powerful driver of new learning and hope. It can connect you with real possibilities for growth, instead of vague goals that may be exciting to look at, but rarely are realized.

By putting your current challenges into a long-range context, you are effectively devoting yourself to today's priorities while also asking, "How does this fit in my overall life and the world around me, now and in the future?"[77] Without such context, we're lost.

When you can see a clear image of the best one-of-a-kind person you could learn to be, then contrast it with current reality. In this clear light of holding in focus, the gap between where you could be and where you are, you can decisively choose what, exactly, you want to stop doing and start doing.

Go ahead and take a quick inventory on a notepad or in your daybook. First, list five things you need to *stop doing* and then list five things you need to *start doing* in order to create the ideal results you want for your life and work five years from today. After each item, write down *when* you will stop or start doing it.

This is how seeing far links in action to seeing near. My grandfather once said to me, "If the stars came out only once in our lifetimes, everyone would be outside to see them and be in absolute awe at the grandeur and wonder of it all. But since the stars shine every night we can go for weeks without ever once looking up at the sky." Seeing far is the counterbalance to living life up close, right now. To succeed in changing conditions, you must be able to see, not just what's in your hand, but also several moves ahead on life's chessboard.

Excelerating

4

Improvise
...to create and enact your own best way forward.

It's healthy now and then to hang a question mark on the things you have taken for granted.
—Bertrand Russell

The essence of improvising is continually exploring new approaches to find what works better, and sometimes abandoning tradition entirely to find your own way.

Years ago, I met an old man on a narrow mountain road in Tibet. My guide and I had come upon a rockslide that completely blocked the old ascending caravan route we were following. It was windy and treacherous. A group of travelers was already beginning to clear the rocks when we stopped to help and inquire how long it would take.

"For more than a thousand years, this has been our path," said a middle-aged woman to my guide as she handed me a rock. I hurled it down the slope and reached for another. Her husband was laboring nearby, and their children had also joined the effort.

An old man approached from the trail below. There was a little girl on his back. "I must get through," he said. "My little one is going to the healer in the village beyond this pass."

"No way through," said one of the others. "The path is closed. You'll have to wait or go back."

I watched the old man survey the scene and then glance beyond the rockslide. At once, he whispered something to the little girl, who clutched his neck more tightly as he gingerly left the established trail and picked his way upward, through the jagged outcroppings into the windy heights. Rocks slid beneath his feet and clattered downward but he chose each handhold with care and sensed a way forward.

"Crazy old man!" cursed one of the caravan men.

"How long do you think it will take for you to clear this?" I asked again.

"Probably, until day's end tomorrow," I was told matter-of-factly.

"Tomorrow?" I watched the light falling and motioned to my guide. We left the trail. Unable to remember the old man's exact path, we made our own. There were moments when my heart caught in my throat as the footing crumbled beneath me, but we moved from one foothold or handhold to the next, and were soon descending into the village beyond.

The next morning I saw the old man and inquired about his granddaughter's well–being. As we talked, I asked him if he often improvised like that, going around the blocked caravan path. He said yes, and I wondered why the others hadn't followed him.

He said, "There are certain times when it's very wise to turn back or wait until you can clear the way. For me, this wasn't one of those times. But that's all most people know. The old ways. The same trail. Sometimes I just need to find my own way."

To a large or small degree, you can often shape what's yet to come, especially if you apply a bit more inventiveness and do the unexpected. Scientists have shown that even a single, small action of ingenuity can get you moving in an effective new direction.[78] You don't have to wait for circumstances to change, resources to be allocated, or someone else to show you the way. Here are several of the small actions that can help you begin improvising more.

- *Identify the path you prefer, and take a different one.* In science, we favor "test loops," the process of making changes that allows you to ascertain immediately whether the new way worked better than the old way. Insert some test loops into your own life. The first step is to become aware of what you've taken for granted. For example, do you always prefer a certain route to work or school? If so, then change it and see what happens. That's improvising. Do you enjoy one kind of exercise or activity more than others? Abandon it once in a while and test an entirely new one. The idea is to find small ways to strengthen your skill at bypassing the brain's inherent change-avoidance tendencies, and then to notice how those variations in your routines are working. When you improvise, you get more curious, and according to medical research you may actually get younger as you get older.[79] Respect tradition—and now and then, break from it.

- *Sometimes, just waiting and thinking is improvising.* In some situations, there is only a split-second to respond. With practiced skills and good instincts, by responding instantly you increase the chances that things will turn out all right. However, for many challenges it's a foolish move to rush right in with the "Answer"—which often turns out to be swift, sure, and wrong.

Instead, once you've calmly faced a new challenge—using the Instant Calming Sequence in Chapter 2, for example—it may be wise to buy a little extra time to get your bearings and let the air clear. This can be the difference between success and failure. The extra moments of waiting can be used to survey the whole landscape, instead of just a small corner of it, discuss the situation with others, or zero in on a few key factors and clarify what matters most to you under these circumstances. Then weigh your options for dealing with things. This strategic hesitation can prove to be one of the most powerful tools for discovering the most effective path to take going forward.

• ***Improvise by drawing one-liners like Picasso.*** A poor student in elementary school, Pablo Picasso was frequently punished by being sent to the "cell," a small room where he sat on a bench for hours, isolated from other students. He made the most of that solitary confinement, taking a pad and paper with him and drawing nonstop. He improvised, never afraid to alter his style or direction in search of a better result, saying later, "What one does with what happens is what counts and not what one has the intention of doing."[80]

One of the simplest ways to appreciate improvising is to take a blank piece of paper and put your pen or pencil on the page in any one spot. Then, without ever lifting the writing instrument off the page, draw a complete picture. It's challenging, fun, and it strengthens how you improvise. Remember the research noted in Chapter 1 about how the hands have extensive "maps" in the brain, and every time you involve new hand movements you promote changes that extend far beyond your fingers.

Want to see some amazing one-liners? Get *Picasso's One-Liners*,[81] a small, delightful sampling of the genius of this artist who turned restriction to his advantage, using his energies to draw instead of mope, and became the most famous and innovative painter of the twentieth century.

• ***Get all your senses involved, not just one.*** When Albert Einstein applied for admission to the Polytechnic Institute in Zurich, he was turned down. As it turned out, that was probably the best thing that could have happened to him. Forced to apply to a lesser institution, Einstein spent a year in the provincial Pestalozzi Institute.

The institute's namesake, the Swiss educator Johann Heinrich Pestalozzi, had been a passionate advocate of learning with the senses. Einstein found himself in an environment where the teachers adhered to Pestalozzi's original assumption that the absolute foundation of knowledge is the ability to observe and improvise.[82]

As taught and practiced at the Pestalozzi Institute, observation meant intense concentration of all the senses and a flexible approach to finding insights or solutions unimpeded by previous knowledge. Students were expected to do far more than read and write. They were asked to observe completely and intently by handling, listening to, and looking at everything they encountered in their day-to-day or classroom experience.

So they didn't begin with the name of something, or a fixed attitude about it. Instead, they first absorbed its properties using their ever-improving powers of observation, and then considered how those observations could be applied in some innovative and meaningful way to help them solve a problem or respond to a challenge.

In all the years that followed, Einstein *applied* this teaching. When he decided on a general direction or subject that interested him, he didn't just dive in, but first released his prior assumptions and got *very* curious about the possibilities, using all of his senses. This is a good example of how excelerating isn't about going faster for its own sake, but about finding a smarter way forward. Then Einstein would pick his own unique way to move forward and make further discoveries. That's improvising—stepping forward with preconceptions left behind and senses fully engaged.

• *Give up something.* I remember when I first learned this lesson long ago: I had just arrived at my grandparents' house on a weekday afternoon following elementary school. I had my book bag on my back, my lunchbox and football in my hands, and my windbreaker tied around my waist. Instead of going straight to the door, I veered off for a quick climb in my favorite tree. It felt like snow was coming, so I figured there was no time to waste.

I set my lunchbox on the ground but tightened the straps to my book bag and stuffed the football inside, not wanting it to get wet. I started up the tree.

Moments later, the first snow came and I realized that I couldn't climb the way I usually did. The tree bark was becoming slick. My feet slid without warning, and my hands slipped. I couldn't get a good hold in the familiar spots. At first, I pretended everything was fine, but after a while I got tired of struggling and climbed down the tree, dejected, snowflakes beginning to accumulate all around me.

My grandfather walked outside and stood beside me, leaning on his cane. He surveyed the scene for a while, not saying anything. Finally he said, "If you want to do something new, you have to stop holding on to everything old."

He nodded to the tree.

I began to climb it again, trying harder this time, which is the natural tendency of the brain's RAS (discussed in the introductory chapter). But it wasn't working, and I found myself getting mad at the tree for the slippery holds. I remember saying, "Awjeez!" which my grandfather didn't like.

"It's not the tree's fault."

"But I can *always* do this!" I replied stubbornly.

"Not today, Robert. There's wind. It's snowing. Conditions are different."

I just looked at him, feeling frustrated.

"Your old habits and all that stuff on your back and around your waist are holding you back. You have to climb a different way today. First you have to give up the things you're carrying."

So I tossed down my jacket and backpack, football and all, to my grandfather, looked for a new handhold, and before the skies opened and more snow came I ended up climbing up higher, and differently, than I ever had. I remember how good it felt.

For me, that was an important lesson about improvising. First, you may have to give up something. If you don't, then the old habits or extra weight will hold you back.

To focus on that letting-go process, write several sentences on a notepad or in your daybook using this model:

To _____ more, _____ less.

Here are some examples that might prime your thinking:

To climb more, carry less.

To hear more, talk less.

To succeed more, assume less.

To invent more, resist less.

To excel more, compete less.

In almost every case of improvising, you can move ahead faster and more freely if you first let go of something.

• ***Champion constructive discontent.*** The earth is flat. No one will ever climb Mt. Everest. No one will ever run a four-minute mile. We will never cure scurvy, diabetes, polio, or diphtheria. People will never fly. Everything that can be invented already has been. Hunger and slavery are inevitable in society. No one will ever reach the moon, let alone walk on it.

A list of that type could include many more examples of limiting beliefs that were all accepted as facts until someone proved them wrong. Cynicism disguises itself as truth and laughs at anything new or different as naïve and foolhardy. Cynicism is about keeping everything the way it was, stifling everything that's different, and calling for endless study before anything new is ever taken seriously—which, effectively, means never. But cynicism has a terrible track record. It's cautious, rigidly resistant—and almost always wrong. It has little place in excelerating.

As William Blake put it, "Without contraries there is no progression." In this world where lots of people keep doing what they've always done and try to please everyone—even though they never can—Blake's words are worth thinking about.

Alfred Sloan, one-time head of General Motors and an icon of American leadership, understood that principle. Once, in a board meeting when an important decision was about to be made, he said, "I take it that everyone is in basic agreement with this decision." All heads in the room nodded in assent. Sloan looked around and said, "Then I suggest we postpone the decision. Until we have some disagreement, we can't fully understand the problem."

To excelerate through a challenge, be sure you seek out the points of friction and consider them, instead of turning away from them. See the good that can come from differing views and experiences. Use the heat of controversy to challenge your own view of what's possible. Stay off balance a bit longer than usual. The Nobel Prize-winning physicist James Franck once remarked that he always recognized a great idea by the feeling of constructive terror that seized him.[83] To improvise, you have to bypass the ancient brain's hold on the status quo. It's emotional. It's disconcerting. And worth it.

• *Change the rules—or the whole game.* When my daughter Shanna was five, she learned to play ping pong. Or should I say, we both learned.

It was early evening after a long day of work pressures for me. I had taken Shanna and my oldest daughter, Chelsea, who was eight, to the nearby recreation center. Chelsea and her friend, Meredith, began playing ping pong. Shanna watched for a while.

Pretty soon she started pestering them to let her play. When they wouldn't, she asked me to go with her to another part of the center. I did. When we returned, the older girls had moved on to another activity and the ping pong table was empty. Shanna asked, "Can we play, Daddy?"

"Sure," I answered.

I spent a few minutes trying to explain what I thought were the simple and basic rules and techniques of the game. Shanna's head was barely above the edge of the table. I tried to imagine that view.

Shanna had the ball and, as kids will do, she started bouncing it off the floor, then throwing it at a nearby chair, and finally swinging her paddle at it, much too hard. After missing it completely on what seemed like fifty swings, she finally hit it and it bounced off the wall and rolled between my feet. She shrieked with laughter.

"No, Shanna, here's the way you do it," I said, demonstrating a proper serve. She swung at it and missed, chasing the bouncing ball and hitting it backwards. It rebounded off the window beside me and sailed past my shoulder. More laughter.

"No, no, Shanna, that's not how you're supposed to do it."

"Who says?"

"Well, a rule book."

"Isn't there another way to play it?"

"No," I answered automatically.

"But who was the person who said that?"

"I don't know."

"Did they have any fun playing it?"

"I'm sure they did..."

"But what if it's more fun another way?" She looked at me expectantly, straight in the eyes.

I hesitated. Here I was, all prepared to follow an instructional checklist. I was making this into a chore, trying to do something old with a little girl who only wanted to have fun and try something new. I stopped myself. My five-year-old was teaching *me*.

That's the power of improvising—not bottled up in intellect or based on preconceived notions. Shanna was choosing her own way to come at this game. I must have looked puzzled or stumped, because she said, "Okay, these are the *new* rules, Daddy!" as she ricocheted the ball off the ceiling and into a distant corner. She squealed with glee. And then I was laughing, too. So were all the adults and children nearby. It was contagious fun, it seemed.

"Let's call this pong ping, Daddy!"

Okay, I thought. It was a good lesson...for me. Sometimes the rules are only as unchangeable as you let them be. Sometimes it's fun to bend or break them—and sometimes at least just to imagine doing so—and see what you learn.

To this day, when our family finishes the evening meal and the weather's too bad to head outside, someone will call for a few minutes of activity, and often it's pong ping. Downstairs we go to chase the little bouncing ball and have some fun together—a new and simple way to have fun that never would have happened if a little girl hadn't decided to improvise.

- *Keep your wits—and wit—about you.* According to researchers, non-hurtful humor is the single fastest way to increase your inventiveness.[84] Laughter is often the shortest distance between two people, from one brain to another. So don't be afraid to lighten up.[85]

Research shows that the most effective leaders in all walks of life use wit more freely, even when things are tense or troubling, and this helps them be more attentive and innovative in finding solutions.[86] Make it a point to keep your humor intact as you improvise a bit more and worry a bit less.

78 *Excelerating*

5

Adapt

...to adjust to new and varying conditions, learning as you go.

We've got to go ahead and jump off the next rise in front of us, adapting our flight to the changing winds.
—Ray Bradbury

I can still see may grandfather standing there, at the end of the dock, in his blue jeans and work shirt, leaning on his cane in the afternoon sun, smiling. It was a long, difficult walk for him as he made his way with me down the steep hill to the water's edge, but I never heard him complain. We just went slowly. It was the last time I went with him to Lake LaSalle before he died.

I was fifteen and he asked me to show him how much my swimming had improved in the past several years. The water was clear as glass, sparkling in the bright light. I picked a new route to swim from the dock around the cattails to the mouth of the creek, then out into the deeper water toward the rocky point and back. I waded through the shallows and kicked my way through the weeds into open water. I always hated the weeds. As usual in this deep, cold lake, I felt icy columns of water jetting up from the many springs on the bottom. I followed my path, swimming freestyle. It all went fine for a while, until I turned into the deep water.

Without warning, the wind whipped up, as it often did when a cold front came gusting along the steep banks above the shoreline. I felt the water surface begin to change but kept heading for the point. Then the whitecaps came and I found myself fighting to stay afloat. Before long, I gave up, turning back toward shore.

"Sorry, grandfather," I said, climbing back on the dock, worn out from the effort. "I hoped to swim farther for you today."

"Why didn't you?" he asked.

"Because the waves came up, and I couldn't. The wind was the problem."

"But the wind was only blowing from one direction. Instead of quitting, why didn't you adapt by changing course so it was at your back, and then you could have kept going?"

I stood there, dripping wet, shivering, thinking about that.

"Watch, the wind is changing again now," he said, pointing. "What if you had stopped to take a quick look around and then swam *with* the wind, from there to *there*?"

What I hadn't noticed from the water I could now see from the dock. There were whitecaps in a few places but only ripples in others. I nodded and went back into the lake. This time I adjusted my stroke and changed course, swimming with the wind behind me, aware of the pull of the currents, trying to streamline more and struggle less. When the waves got higher I stopped fighting them and lifted my head above the water, gauging the best way to alter my stroke or vary my course. This time when I finally swam back to the dock I crossed the waves at an angle instead of plowing directly into them.

I've never forgotten what I learned that day.

As Heraclitus put it, "How one meets change reveals all." Once you start out on a new course, no matter how well conceived, conditions tend to shift along the way, often unexpectedly. Improvising is fine, but sometimes we get partway into it and conditions change in ways we never anticipated. That's when we need to adapt, and probably keep adapting, cycling our attention between action and interpretation and then new action. To do that, you have to see past your own plans, or at least hold them lightly and realize that at best, they may only partially come true as you initially imagined. The problem with plans is that they are often too wishful in eliminating what we don't want and determining our actions as if life itself were predictable and controllable.

Strategic expert Henry Mintzberg calls this shortcoming the "fallacy of predetermination."[87] Business strategy has long been founded on the notion that we can predict the future and influence its course through our vision and action. But the truth is, we can't predict the future, and while we can set out an innovative course going forward, we don't know what's going to happen next.

There are two basic ways to adapt and it's important to recognize the difference. One way is by taking what I call the *low road*: tensing up, hunkering down, getting defensive, stonewalling, tuning out, while you try to keep doing the same thing you were doing only harder and faster. Although this may help you to cope or at least survive, if you repeatedly adapt in that way your mind and body become reshaped over time by what researchers call the "general adaptation syndrome"—a process that increases tension and resistance (which soon feel "normal") and leads to exhaustion.[88] On the low road, you can end up impervious to learning and blocked from growth, wishing things would just cooperate and go back to what you expected earlier on.

That's not the adapting I'm talking about. On the *high road*, you are aware of changing conditions as you go forward, and adapt to them by remaining open and nondefensive and making continuing adjustments in your approach. As evolution has shown us, it's not the strongest that survive, nor the most intelligent, but those that are most adaptive to change: those who excelerate.[89]

Make Surprise Your Ally

It's remarkable how many times in life we're faced with the fact that what used to work doesn't work anymore. The fast, flowing form of human intelligence that solves new problems with new solutions is called *fluid* intelligence, while habitual patterns of trying to resist change and solve new problems with old solutions are labeled *crystallized* intelligence.[90] To increase your ability to fluidly adapt to changing conditions, you can apply some of the strategies that were discussed in the preceding chapter, and supplement them with the others described here.

• *Adapt by Anticipating Change.* If all we try to do is manage the unexpected after it happens, we're always playing catch-up. Whenever possible, we have to use our intuition and senses to anticipate the unexpected, so we're better able to adjust to it or to catch errors in their earliest moments, before they build.

Excelerating requires that you remain curious, flexible, nimble, and attentive, with your senses helping you gauge what's coming so you can adapt when you need to—or even sooner. One way to develop your anticipatory skill is to notice "All because of..." experiences. Consider the following poem, written by an eight-year-old:

> **All because of...**
> *One day a bumblebee flew in the window.*
> *Little Sally yelled.*
> *Her father jumped up to swat the bee but tipped over the chair.*
> *The chair toppled the telephone,*
> *Which beeped "911."*

The operator heard yelling and sent the police.
Who didn't arrive before
The father swatted at the buzzing bee and
Missed, but hit the curtain which fell on the cat
Who screeched and jumped onto the kitchen table
Which knocked over Sally's birthday cake
And the candles caught the newspaper on fire
Which set off the smoke alarm
Which called the fire department
Which sent a big red fire truck, with sirens blaring.
The little boy yelled "Cool!" at all the commotion
And started running around the kitchen.
The mom did not know what to do so she gave the little boy a toy
Which was when the neighbors saw the police and fire trucks
Rushing down the street.
But the fire went out by itself
And all the neighbors gathered on the lawn
As the family sighed with relief
And no one even noticed
The little bumblebee zipping out the window
And flying away.
THE END.

The author? My youngest daughter, Shanna. Time required: about five minutes. I know, because she wrote the whole thing while sitting in my office. She has already realized that life is largely a mosaic of "All because of…" experiences. We start something, and then the unexpected happens and, if we adapt and keep going, one thing leads to another, into a series of new experiences, or new laughter, or deeper into life.

"Inventors of the future must be poets," said Thomas Edison, "so they can see what others often miss."[91] If you were to write your own "All because of…" explanation about the cause-and-effect background to a challenge you're facing, what would it say? Follow Edison's advice and be a poet, at least briefly.

Do this by thinking about one example that applies to your work and another example that fits life beyond the job. Just for practice—and the fun of it—think of an irrationally hopeful or wildly successful outcome to each of those stories. If you were lucky, and a couple of unexpectedly positive things happened along the way, how could it turn out? Now think back through the causal steps that could actually make that happen. Jot them down in two "All because of a…" poems.

Now think about them. How could you change your own old reactive habits into new responses so that there's a better chance of a more successful outcome? By rehearsing in your mind a string of events, some of which you can control and some of which you can't, you strengthen your adapting skills. You can always exert some influence over your own responses, which then influences what happens next. By adapting as you go, and rehearsing through a series of causal steps and your adjustments to them, you will usually end up with far better results than you would have had on autopilot, no matter what the circumstance.

What if you were starting an important project in a new way and, without warning, you received a phone call that triggered a whole series of changes? How would you adapt? Or what if there was a sudden change in the health of a loved one and, in turn, this called for changes in your schedule and life? How might thinking in advance about the possibilities and your positive reactions change the way you handle things?

It's important to remember that you are always preparing yourself for the next challenge. Every time you practice, or even imagine, a new way of observing and adapting, you strengthen key brain areas that improve your chances for responding better the next time. To sharpen your adapting abilities, you might do as I do and post a small index card reading "All because of..." in an area where you spend quite a bit of time. Use it as a reminder to more closely observe how often a single small change can produce a lasting series of cause-and-effect results. Your whole day can turn on a dime, as the saying goes.

- ***When something stops working, get really curious, really fast.*** Lots of us are experts at becoming defensive whenever something goes wrong—it wasn't my fault, and here are all the reasons that my approach should still be working, even though it isn't. That typical reaction wastes time and energy. It distracts you from getting ingenious and acting quickly to make new progress.

I remember a fellow Marine who was trying to pitch his tent on a rocky hillside on a stormy night during our advanced combat training for the Vietnam War. He had climbed higher on the slope and discovered what appeared to be an ideal site for his tent, providing a defensible line of sight. He had improvised. So far, so good.

But then the fog came in from the ocean. He couldn't see. He was so committed to his site, however, that he remained there for quite a while, cursing under his breath, shielding his eyes in hopes that the fog would magically clear and he could have the best view again. No such luck.

Finally an old gunnery sergeant, just back from the war, walked over and said, "Son, there are times when you have to be willing to pitch your tent somewhere else."

Observe yourself the next time you're being innovative, and then something doesn't go right. Can you remain open and non-defensive, and get really curious, really fast? Can you devote all your energy to making an adjustment and testing it to see if it works?

You might also set up some practice sessions for yourself in adapting to sudden and unexpected changes. Pick a game that you usually play by the rules. Then, in mid-game, when you least expect it, complicate things so you are forced to adapt as you go. If you're playing basketball, tennis, soccer, volleyball, or ping pong, you might have someone toss a second ball into play, or keep going after dark or by suddenly turning out the lights, or create tag-teams that randomly substitute for each other while the game keeps going. You get the idea. By the way, there is medical evidence that such novel experiences not only make us more adaptable, they can actually help slow or reverse many aspects of biological aging in the brain and body.[92]

• *Sense the line of incoming energy and adapt to it.* I have studied, practiced, and taught martial arts since I was young. There's a simple exercise that has had a lot of carryover value into my life and work, and I believe you may find it helpful, too.

Every challenging situation has a primary *line of energy*. By sensing that line, you can adapt by moving out of the way instead of getting bowled over. You have many choices about how to react to the incoming force. Imagine yourself standing on a compass, as illustrated.

The Incoming Challenge: Words, Action, or Situation

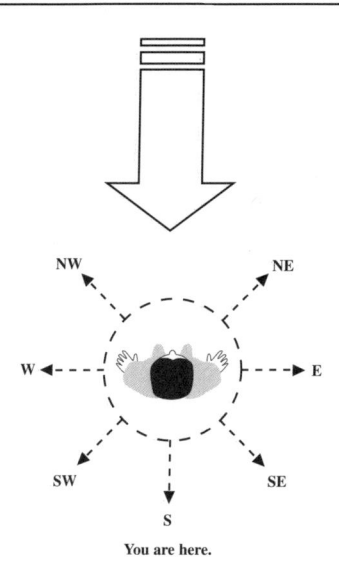

NW   NE

W ◄ - - - - ► E

SW   SE
S

You are here.

If you freeze up and don't adapt at all, the change or challenge will collide with you head-on. At the least that will leave you disoriented. You adapt by moving off the direct line of force, sidestepping it. From this new position you can more calmly observe what's going on and choose how to evade the incoming force (with a clarifying question or small action, for example) or deflect it (with a de-escalating word). You retain calm control, and such control can dramatically change the outcome. You might also sense whether you should step toward the line before it gathers too much force, or perhaps step farther back and see if it dissipates before reaching you.

Go ahead and try it now.

To make this approach instinctive you have to practice it. Place yourself in the diagram and imagine what the effects will be if you do not move out of the direct line of energy. Then imagine how you could step aside from that line, and what the implications of doing so might be. Don't fail to consider the possibility that you could align yourself completely with that energy, and that by doing so it might propel you more quickly to an outcome you desire.

• *Study examples of people who adapt well to changing circumstances.* General George Patton advised, "The best way to prepare for the unknown is by studying how others in the past have adapted to the unforeseeable and the unpredictable."[93] Thomas Edison once remarked, "The real measure of success is more than taking a new direction, it's endlessly adapting as you go."[94]

I have appreciated the chances I have had over the years to observe and learn from leaders in action from all walks of life. Research shows that paying attention to models of exceptional performance under pressure can be of great value.[95]

Take notes. Think about the most exceptional people you have known. How have they risen to the occasion in facing changing conditions? Jotting down your impressions of such people in a daybook is a good way to deepen learning and have a convenient way to recall these examples from time to time. Assemble books and articles that help you better understand the vast untapped potential that we each have for adapting to change in ways that create results that really matter.[96]

• *Know when to adapt by leaving the challenge behind.* "Challenging your edges" is an expression used by rock climbers. Doing so is a useful way to test your capabilities beyond what you usually do or are already good at doing. But there's a moment when challenging our edges can push us over the edge. We all know the feeling, summed up in a little poem I learned long ago:

It's usually not the big things that
drive a person crazy...
not a lost dream
or a lost heart
but a shoelace that snaps
with no time left...

When you find yourself in this place—where you've suddenly gone beyond challenging your edges and are now over the edge—take action. Apply the ICS in Chapter 2. Note that in certain situations it may not be enough by itself. When that happens, the first thing to do is to take responsibility for your overreaction—that is, admit it instead of trying to justify your outrage or stuff it all inside, insisting that you're actually doing just fine, thank you. You might say something like, "Okay, *now* I'm over the edge. I don't like it, but I am." A bit of non-hurtful humor here—laughing at your own reactions—can go a long way in helping you and others cope with this and move on. You may need to step away from the challenge for a while or do something else to regain your bearings and come at it anew.

There are several other well-proven ways to adapt by doing something that briefly separates you from a problem while boosting your energy and resilience, such as:

- **✦ Get moving.** Physical movement helps flood the brain with endorphins that raise mood and provide increased resilience in tough situations. As little as five minutes of light physical activity—a walk outside may be best, or climbing a few flights of stairs, or even pacing back and forth in front of a window—can help shift your physiology toward positive control. Going for walks can help lessen feelings of anger or frustration, and may also increase your empathic capacity to see things from other people's viewpoints.[97]

Cardiologists have found that exercise seems to eliminate excess stress chemicals by using them for energy expressed outwardly rather than harming the body internally.[98] You might also drink some ice water or tea, eat a healthy snack, get some bright light, or listen to pleasant music. Experiment to find what works best for you.

✦ **Write things down.** The act of writing about an experience has been shown to reduce negative emotions and create heightened ability to deal with adversity. Research indicates that those who write about traumatic events for 20 minutes a day for four consecutive days—if possible, soon after the events—have significantly more robust immune systems and report less distress than the people who do no writing.[99]

✦ **Talk it through.** For some people, talking with others about a difficult situation is a productive pattern of coping with adversity.[100] It can help release tensions, reestablish perspective, and confirm that you have solid social support, no matter how tough things may be right now.

✦ **Help someone else in need.** Empathy has immense—and often immediate—power to help us cope with our own difficulties. Go spend some time helping someone whose challenges are bigger than yours. Spend an evening helping homeless families, or mentally challenged children, or nursing home residents. By doing good for them you are also helping regain your own perspective.

✦ **Take a new view.** Think of what matters most to you, and why you're making the efforts you are, even when adversity sometimes gets in the way for a while. Imagine yourself gazing at the stars or standing on the beach at sunrise, or enjoying a view of one of your favorite hilltops or mountains. You might also recall the person you have known in your life who has lost or suffered the most and still made a positive difference in the lives of others.

• *Feel the fear and keep changing anyway.* Because the brain is programmed to assume the worst, a dilemma can often appear worse than it is. Giving in to that inaccurate perception can put you into a negative spiral of helplessness and inadequacy. As Aristotle said, "We become brave by taking brave actions." Adapting makes us brave. So feel the fear and adapt anyway.

In a wonderful book called *Grow or Die: The Unifying Principle of Transformation*, biologist George Land cites extensive scientific research showing that at every moment, every cell in the body is either growing or dying. There is no staying the same, no matter how hard you try. "The nature of a cell, just like what we call 'human nature,' is not something that *is*, but something forever in the process of *becoming*. If conditions and feedback permit new growth patterns, the result will be growth. If not, the result will be regression."[101]

It was Aristotle who said, "Time does not exist except for change." The origin of the word change is the Old English *cambium*, which means "becoming." Time does not exist except for becoming something new. That's what adapting helps you do—to do the best you can, with what you have, wherever you are.

Ask yourself, "What can I do, however small, to adjust what I'm doing and adapt a bit more to gain some control over what happens next?" Use the techniques described in this book to give yourself the best chance of succeeding. Remember that each time you create an anchor, or apply the Instant Calming Sequence, or use all your senses, or take any other constructive step, you are also redefining your brain and body pathways so you excelerate more effectively through the next challenge.

> *I sense it coming but cannot avoid it.*
> *My boat strikes something.*
> *At first sounds of silence, waves.*
> *Nothing has happened;*
> *Or perhaps everything has happened*
> *And I am sitting in my new life.*
> —Rumi

6

Overcome

...to persevere and keep growing, giving the world the best you have.

> *Approach what you find most difficult.*
> *Help those you think you cannot help.*
> *Release what you are clinging to.*
> *Go to places that scare you. Grow and overcome.*
> —Script from a rock carving in Central Tibet[102]

Just before the final turn, right when many people are ready to overcome adversity, they quit. Time and again, they struggle with a challenge for a while, but ultimately give up or give in. Sometimes that may be wise. Often it's not. Knowing the difference can make all the difference.

History teaches us all that there is no advancement without toil, no progress without perseverance, no growth without uncertainty, no triumph without the readiness to risk defeat. When I work with leaders I ask them to answer two questions—which you might also answer right now:

1. Briefly describe one of the greatest successes in your life or work.

2. Briefly describe one of the greatest setbacks in your life or work.

I usually suggest that people *not* list their most personally painful events, such as a divorce or the death of a loved one; there are usually many other adversities to choose from, and for the first steps of solid development to occur it is best to start on the safer ground of something less devastating.

Then I ask a follow-up question:

Which of the above examples has had the most significant influence in shaping who you are today as a leader or a person—and why?

If you are like the vast majority of individuals I have worked with, you probably said that a certain setback had the most positive effect on you.

I have answered those questions many times myself. Doing so always reminds me that I have a long list of stumbles and falls, and my list of successes always pales in comparison. By the way, most people don't list business successes or professional achievements. They usually list personal successes such as raising a child, caring for an ill parent, earning the money for their own schooling, helping someone in need, coaching in a community education program, or helping out at a church.

On the adversity side, there is an astonishing range of setbacks that have made a difference, and we can only realize that when we bring them into the light for examination and reflection. As Theodore Roethke put it, "In a dark time, the eye begins to see."

The spirit of overcoming is in all of us, although sometimes its light grows dim. It calls on us to create our own means of ultimately becoming our best, whatever life brings.

"Great spirits meet calamity greatly," Aeschylus wrote. In many situations, the small actions of overcoming happen quietly, across time, and no one else may ever know. There are also times when it takes every ounce of courage we can muster. "Look at a man in the midst of doubt and danger, and you will learn in his hour of adversity what he really is," said the Roman philosopher Lucretius. "It is then that true utterances are wrung from the recesses of the heart. The mask is torn off; the reality remains."

When Everything Goes Dead Wrong

To survive the constant battle with the unexpected, two qualities are indispensable: first, a mind that even in this moment of intense darkness retains some trace of the inner light that will lead it forward and, second, the courage to go where that faint light leads.

—Karl von Clausewitz

From the time I was very young I have been interested in the stories of people who stepped forward to face the most difficult challenges life can bring and who overcame the worst kinds of adversity. Some of that interest undoubtedly began with the question that my grandfather asked me when he told me his own story of surviving the raging fire that had trapped him and my grandmother. "If you were standing right here and a fire came, what would you do?" Whenever I read or hear an account of someone who succeeded against terrible odds, I ask myself, "What would I have done?"

You might ask yourself that same question about a true account that goes way back to China in the third century B.C.E.[103] It is the story of Sun Bin, who as a young man was known as Master Sun, or Sun Tzu II. He was the grandson of General Sun Tzu, who wrote the strategy classic, *The Art of War*.

Sun Bin lived during the Era of the Warring States, a time of chaos and brutal competition, not so unlike today in many areas of the world. According to the traditional anthology known as Strategies of the Warring States:[104]

> Usurpers set themselves up as lords and kings; states that were run by pretenders and plotters established armies to make themselves into major powers. They imitated each other at this more and more, and those who came after them also followed their example.

> Eventually, they overwhelmed and destroyed one another, conspiring with larger domains to annex smaller domains, spending years at violent military operations, filling the fields with blood.
>
> Fathers and sons were alienated, brothers were at odds, husbands and wives were estranged. No one could safeguard his or her life. Integrity disappeared. Eventually things reached the chaotic extreme where seven large states and five smaller states contested with each other for power, forming unstable and ever-shifting alliances in the pursuit of greed and personal ambition.

Young Master Sun studied warfare and strategy, along with a fellow student named Pang Juan, under the mysterious sage Wang Li, author of one of the most intricate and sophisticated of strategic classics.[105] Pang Juan was hired by the court of the state of Wei, where he was given the rank of general. Aware that his own abilities as a strategist were not equal to those of Master Sun, Pang Juan conspired to eliminate him. He invited Master Sun to Wei on the pretext of consulting with him. When Master Sun arrived, Pang Juan had him arrested as a criminal and condemned him to the severest torture. Both of Master Sun's feet were cut off and his face was horribly disfigured—a punishment designed to reduce a person to the status of permanent outcast. From that day onwards he was known as Sun Bin—"Sun the Mutilated."

His story was far from over, however. Sun Bin possessed a deep and abiding sense of his own unique worthiness as a person. He believed that he could still make a difference with his life, despite this horrible setback and the treachery and terror around him. Perhaps he could still find a way to ultimately unify the Warring States. Whatever it was, in his darkest hour he found the drive to transcend his tortured self. While still imprisoned, he managed to gain a brief, private audience with an emissary from the state of Qi.

Although hideously maimed and in excruciating pain, Sun Bin quickly astounded the envoy—who had to exert his own calmness and toughness not to turn away from Sun Bin—with his courage and obvious wisdom about strategy and warfare. The emissary sensed a solidity, not so much from the strength of his body—with its layered maze of hideous scars where once had been a handsome face, head, and neck—as from the sureness of his heart and ideas. Recognizing the value of such an ally, the emissary smuggled Sun Bin out of prison and into his own state of Qi, where Sun Bin soon proved himself and was appointed strategist and military consultant to the famed general Tian Ji.[106]

Sun Bin's tactics, centered on securing victory with minimal harm and at minimal cost, eventually changed the nature of war. If possible, both sides would end the conflict without humiliation. His teachings, entitled *The Lost Art of War*, were indeed lost for nearly 2,000 years until a nearly complete version, recorded on 232 small bamboo tablets, was discovered in 1972 in an ancient tomb in Shangdong Province. His metaphors—and his extraordinary personal example—can be applied to many life events other than warfare. We must know ourselves, know our challenges, and then commit to overcoming them in constructive ways—by excelerating.

Turning Bad into Good

Ask anyone who's a veteran of life's battles, and you will likely hear that the only one in the world who can defeat you is…you. Throughout this book I have suggested small actions that can help sustain your perseverance during difficult times. Here are some additional insights and tools for you to consider.

- ***Remember the hardships you have overcome, and learn how others have prevailed.*** Consider this simple and enduring question: "When your children, grandchildren, nieces and nephews take their place in the world and you say to them, 'I was at the point of difficulty and danger, and I did this...' what will you describe?"

As I mentioned in the previous chapter, become more aware of how you persevere and overcome, in ways large and small. Read about men and women who exemplify this spirit, and talk about it with the people closest to you. You will likely be surprised by how much your loved ones and friends have endured and overcome, things you never knew before.

- ***Pause every morning to remember why you're getting out of bed.*** It's a simple choice, really, but one that most of us miss: a few extra moments of soul-searching before stepping out of bed and facing the day. I've heard from leaders for many years that this is one of their great little mobilizing actions, because few things re-invigorate the spirit more than knowing that even if you find yourself in a really rough patch today on life's highway, you're going to overcome it for something—or someone—greater than just yourself. Remember, your inner fire is not somewhere *out there*; it's *in here*, always close by, waiting for you to claim it each day, and at every challenge, anew.

- ***When you come up against the next wall, invent a way to get beyond it.*** Walls are everywhere. Sometimes you can climb over them. Other times, you have to find a way around them or take them down, stone by stone. However, wishing they weren't there, arguing that they shouldn't be there, or hoping that someone else will remove them only increases the resistance they produce. Our progress in life and work often hinges on how we handle the walls along the way.

There's a rock climbing gym not far from my home. I enjoy going there and taking my children there, not just for the exercise but for the way it tests and toughens our calmness and vision. It requires that we each keep testing and applying our own ways to improvise, adapt, and overcome.

Sometimes it's very hard at the end of a long day to be standing there on the ground looking up at all the obstacles in the way on the walls—the rock outcroppings, twisting overhangs, and long shadowy gaps. These are the moments when I think, with a smile, that it would have been better to go home instead. But, if I get past that initial feeling of the enormity of the challenge, I can then look from one obstacle to the next. Many times, the obstacles themselves reveal a way upward, around one and over another, across difficult passages that, at first glance, seemed well beyond reach.

It amazes me how quickly and easily children can learn such skills and begin to pick their path upward with little fear. They can work their way sideways along vertical walls, reach for difficult holds, and cross barriers that appear insurmountable from the ground.

Think of a wall in your life or work, some existing or probable barrier between where you are and where you want to be. It might be lack of money, resources, job title, authority, education, even luck. Remember the saying that luck is when preparation and ingenuity meet opportunity. Walls are opportunities, but only if we can learn to see them that way.

Consider why it's such a big barrier. Perhaps because it's too high, steep, dark, slippery, rough, risky, unfair...you know the list.

But then, for the sake of this exercise, come up with one small thing that might work in overcoming it. If this exercise is hard for you then you might just think of something really far-fetched:

a gust a wind might lift you up, the wall might fall down on its own. But then be very pragmatic: *If there was one thing, no matter how small, that I could do right now to make progress in getting past this wall, it would be...* It could be anything: a little more hand or leg strength, a better way to see past the next handhold, or deciding to climb around it instead of straight upward, or teaming up with a friend instead of going it all alone. Maybe there *is* a way!

• ***Be an alchemist.*** Sometimes it really pays to go in exactly the opposite direction that others are going and see what happens. The jazz great Duke Ellington summed it up when he said, "I merely took the energy it takes to pout and played some blues." How can you transform negative or unproductive energy into something improbable and positive? That's another form of overcoming.

• ***Imagine that children are watching you.*** This small tool always makes me stop and think. In my work with leaders, I ask them to create an ideal laboratory for a person to do what's right and to pass on to others the values that truly matter. Often this description includes being in a room where young children are watching and listening, assessing and absorbing every word, idea, feeling, and action. There's no separation in that room between what's acceptable at work or among adults and what's all right as a lesson to young people.

Children—and adults, too—learn very little from what we say. But they learn a lot from what they feel from us and how they see us behave under pressure. What if the ways you face every hardship and deal with every problem were being observed by a group of youngsters—your own children and their friends, perhaps. How would you want them to view you? What would you want them to learn from you and say about you?

- ***Box up your setbacks, mistakes, and losses—and keep them in perspective.*** Another simple, very useful tool is to practice putting setbacks in their place. That is, quickly visualize where you are on a two-axis chart as shown below. The vertical line on the left side of the page represents the best of who you are—your distinguishing qualities, values, strengths, and passions. The horizontal line across the top is all the difference your life has made in the world, from birth through today and on into the future.

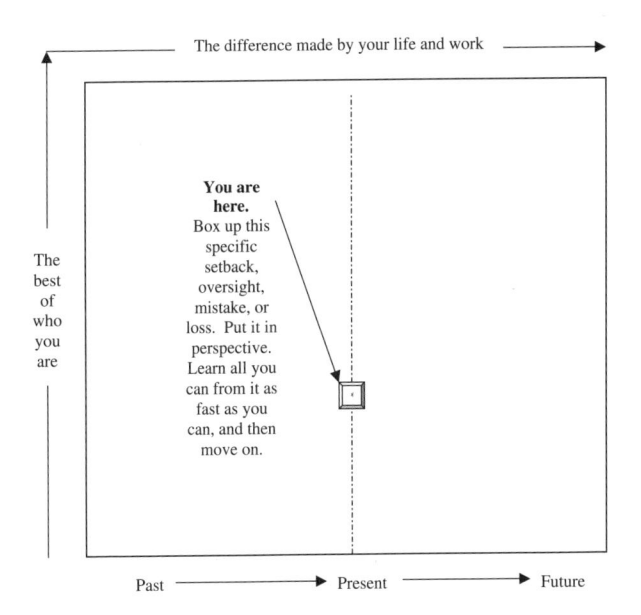

The difference made by your life and work

You are here.
Box up this specific setback, oversight, mistake, or loss. Put it in perspective. Learn all you can from it as fast as you can, and then move on.

The best of who you are

Past → Present → Future

Put your current problem or setback in a small, defined box in the middle of this landscape of who you are, the work you love to do, the people you love and care about, the differences you have worked to make, and the overall integrity of your life's message. We all make mistakes. We all fall, occasionally many times in a row. But if we develop more constructive responses to every stumble and plummet, we begin to change our own brain structure and function—and then we can bounce back faster from future setbacks and emerge stronger and more dedicated to what really matters. Put it in perspective, learn everything you can from each slip and fall as quickly as you can, and then move on.

- ***Rehearse overcoming adversity.*** Aristotle believed courage to be foremost among human virtues, because it strengthens all the others or makes them possible. You can build courage through mental rehearsal. Imagine being in a very tough situation, on the brink of overcoming but not there yet. Notice what makes you anxious, or doubtful, and what thoughts or feelings you can generate that overcome this fearful or tentative reaction. This is a way to assemble what you need most to face really hard situations at your best.

There is no one formula that works for everyone. Control your breathing—slow and deep—and stay very focused on this current moment (see yourself on the verge of overcoming, not failing). Envision your success. Remember what you love about overcoming things and practice summoning those images, calling upon the most powerful reminders of what is meaningful to you, such as the smiles of loved ones and friends, the view at the top of the climb, or the feeling of inner satisfaction that this was an effort worth making. Those who consistently overcome difficulties in a wide range of work and life situations have developed their own inner tool kit to draw upon. It's an important step to take—before you need it.

- ***Build forward.*** As Emerson reminded us, "Life is a succession of lessons, which must be lived to be understood." Among the difficulties that I have faced, one in particular relates to the fact that you are reading this book.

Years ago, I was awarded a contract from a publishing house to write my third nonfiction book. I spent nearly a year doing the research and early drafts. I took a number of risks, both in writing style and format.

It was exciting. I had improvised a new approach to the subject. I was adapting my writing as new research findings appeared, trying to develop a new way to help my readers get the most value out of the book, as easily as possible.

In all, I invested nearly a year of my life, going through six complete rewrites in close cooperation with my senior editor. She was pleased with the new direction the book was creating. We both believed it worked. At last I submitted the finished draft to her, and she sent a copy to her boss, the editor-in-chief.

He read it over the weekend and on Monday he rejected it.

More than that, he rejected me as an author. He said my experimental style, conversational tone, and writing format were all failures, a disgrace to what he called "the fine traditions of nonfiction writing." He added: "I'm from an Ivy League school. I know about writing, and Robert Cooper can't write."

He informed my editor that he was killing the book. He ordered her to terminate my contract, even though it contained a clause that gave me the right to rewrite the book based on input from the editor and editor-in-chief. He instructed the accounting department not to pay the money that was owed to me for my work that year.

Finally, he ordered my editor not to call me, but instead to inform me of all this in a fax. I remember sitting alone in my office as the fax was printing out, then walking over to pick it up, holding it in my hands as I read each line.

This setback not only affected me, it affected my whole family. I might have been able to walk away from it when I was young and single, but by then I had piles of bills, a mortgage, very little savings, and a family with young children who were counting on me. It was right before the December holidays. I was stunned and suddenly broke.

I felt the weight of the world on my shoulders. It seemed that I had completely let my family down. What would I do next? After mulling things over for a while, I left the office and went home to face my wife, Leslie, and the children, to tell them we would have to find another way to keep going financially. I knew they would be watching how I handled this. Challenges are both a test and a tool.

I remember sitting with them and trying to explain what had happened. I will never forget Leslie's response. It wasn't about our need for money, or the bitterness of this setback after all the long hours of work; it wasn't even about the callousness of that editor and his reprehensible treatment of someone who had given every ounce of his best to complete a job.

It was about what, looking back years later, matters beneath everything else at times like this. Leslie held my hand and looked into my eyes. All she said was, "Are you going to listen to him? Are you going to stop writing?"

I remember looking at her in the kind of amazement we feel for those who love us so deeply that they know our souls, sometimes better than we know them ourselves. She sensed that the fundamental issue in all this was about overcoming a punishing setback to continue doing what really mattered to me, the work that most completely engaged my heart, mind, and spirit. She knew that together we would find other ways to make a living and provide for our family. We would not take to heart the words of an Ivy League literary authority. And we would not give up.

Are you going to listen to him? Are you going to stop writing?

You hold in your hands my eleventh book.

Excelerating

Final Thoughts

When Your Moment Comes

There always comes a moment in time when a door opens and lets the future in.
—Graham Greene

Whenever we face a new challenge, we are given a chance to learn from it as a way to uncover hidden capacity and become better at excelerating toward our true priorities. At times like these, we are given the opportunity to shape the person we want to be instead of settling for what we are right now or have always been.

The past is over and the future isn't here yet. This moment is the one filled with the greatest promise.

In my family, it is a tradition that each New Year's Eve one of us will say a few words about what we've learned from times past and all that we hope for in the days to come.

Last year, I wrote a short poem that captured some of my wishes for every individual, young or old, who is ready to meet adversity with calm effectiveness and create success on his or her own terms. Just before midnight, surrounded by family and friends, I read the words aloud, ending with the following challenge to us all:

When your moment comes,
> *remember that the biggest risk in life is not to risk at all*
> *and a single act of courage*
> *is more powerful than all the cynics and complainers rolled into one.*

When your moment comes,
> *it may not be what you planned*
> *and it may be more challenging than you ever imagined,*
> *but remember that you have a destiny beckoning to be lived,*
> *and you can't count on reinforcements,*
> *can't wait for conditions to be just right,*
> *can't expect a miracle,*
> *can't settle for less,*
> *can't play it safe,*
> *can't sit this one out,*
> *can't turn away…*

When your moment comes—
Now, right here, in your hands.

Acknowledgments

This work has been many years in the making.

Excelerating is a concept that I first began exploring in the 1980s. I searched far and wide to find insights and answers that not only made sense but were practical to apply. Whatever value is held on these pages owes much to the generous contributions of the many wise and caring individuals who have helped me keep my mind open and my feet on the ground through the years.

First, I thank God and the Powers of Light and Love, and my immediate family: my wife, Leslie, for her enduring love and the opportunity to share our lives, and my children, Chris, Chelsea, and Shanna, for your love and inspiration.

I thank my father, Hugh, my mother, Margaret, and my grandparents, Hugh and Nora Cooper, and Wendell and Marion Downing, for the many lessons and questions you have passed on to me.

I also thank my sister, Mary, her husband, Pedro, and their children: Andie, Becky, and Tricia; and my brother, David, his wife, Nanette, and their children: Nate and Anna Marie.

In all phases of writing I have relied on the wisdom and support of an exceptional circle of friends, including:

Jerry de Jaager, whose keen editorial insights guided this work into its final form.

Suanne Sandage, whose professional talents and initiative have been amazing.

Julie Ross, whose video production gifts are second to none.

Larry Taylor, whose leadership discussions and big heart have meant so much.

Deborah Kiley, whose partnership with me in developing exceptional leaders over the past decade has been a highpoint of my work.

Other friends and colleagues who also read and commented on the early drafts of this book, including (alphabetically): Connie Bever, LuAnn Freund, Kimberly LeRoy, Duane and Alpha Sandage, and Nan Summers.

And (alphabetically): Julie Anixter, Nancy Badore, Jeff Bergeron, Tony Condi, Elly Rose Cooper, Bruce Cryer, Deb DeHaas, Brian Doty, Susan Duggan, Howie Engle, John Fayad, Tom Fischer, Alan Fox, Josh Freedman, Hans-Gerd Füchtenkort, Ruth and Norman Hapgood, Bob Hardcastle, Mary Hershberger, Alan Horton, John Horton, Michael Hoppé, Mary "Bunny" Huller, Larry Katzen, Dan Kiley, John and Marcia Kulick, Paul Laughlin, Helen Lemmon, Jim Loehr, Dan and Roberta Marsh, Susan Marshall, Esther Orioli, Michael Ray, Heidi Ream, Charlotte Roberts, Paul Sanders, Ayman and Rowan Sawaf, Howard and Linda Schultz, Dawn Sorenson, Sandy Stafford, Jim Stockdale, Stephanie and Phil Tade, Lynn Taylor, Nettie Van Allstine, Sirah Vettese, Chad and Kristine Walker, Bob and Tina Webster, Jeff Willett, and Kathryn Young.

And to all the other wise and caring people who have shined a light for me along the way.

Notes

[1] For many years I carried in my wallet a small 1921 newspaper article that reported this incident. Headlined "Man Survives by Swimming through Fire," it reads in its entirety: "Forest fires broke out last week in several areas near the state park. Neighbors report that an unnamed man stayed alive by swimming in a creek when a fire swept through the forest near his home."

[2] See, for example: Weick, K., and Roberts, K. "Collective Mind in Organizations: Heedful Interacting on Flight Decks." *Administrative Science Quarterly* 38(1993): 357-381.

[3] See, for example: Kegan, R., and Lahey, L.L. *How the Way We Talk Can Change the Way We Work* (San Francisco: Jossey-Bass, 2001).

[4] My previous works include: Cooper, R.K. *The Other 90%: How to Unlock Your Vast Untapped Potential for Leadership and Life* (New York: Crown Business, 2001). For an excellent introduction to the practical workings of the brain, see, for example: Carter, R. *Mapping the Mind* (Berkeley: University of California Press, 1998); Amen, D.G. *Change Your Brain, Change Your Life* (New York: Times Books, 1998); Ornstein, R. *The Evolution of Consciousness* (New York: Prentice Hall, 1991); Ornstein, R. *The Right Mind* (New York: Harcourt Brace, 1997); Lawrence, P.R., and Nohria, N. *Driven* (San Francisco: Jossey-Bass, 2002); and Wilson, R.A., and Keil, F.C. (Eds.) *The MIT Encyclopedia of the Cognitive Sciences* (Cambridge, MA: MIT Press, 1999).

[5] See for example: Restak, R. *Mozart's Brain and the Fighter Pilot* (New York: Harmony Books, 2001).

[6] See, for example: Zull, J.E. *The Art of Changing a Brain: Helping People Learn by Understanding How the Brain Works* (Sterling, VA: Stylus, 2002); and Amen. *Change Your Brain, Change Your Life*.

[7] See, for example: Hardin, P.P. *What Are You Doing with the Rest of Your Life?* (Novato, CA: New World Library, 1992); Erikson, E. *Identity and the Life Cycle* (New York: Norton, 1994); McAdams, D.P., and De St. Aubin, E. (Eds.)

Generativity and Adult Development (New York: American Psychological Association, 1998); McAdams, D.P., Josselson, R., and Lieblich, A. (Eds.) *Turns in the Road* (New York: American Psychological Association, 2001).

[8] Loehr, J., and Schwartz, T. "The Making of a Corporate Athlete." *Harvard Business Review* (Nov., 2000): 120-128.

[9] See, for example: Lewise, T., Amini, F, and Lannon, R. *A General Theory of Love* (New York: Random House, 2000).

[10] Kreiman, G., Koch, C., and Fried, I. "Imagery Neurons in the Human Brain." *Nature* 408(2000): 357-361.

[11] Carter, C., et al. "How the Brain Gets Ready to Perform." (Lecture at the 30th Annual Meeting of the Society of Neuroscience, New Orleans, Nov., 2000).

[12] Schweitzer, A. Quoted in Franck, F. (Ed.) *What Does It Mean to be Human?* (New York: St. Martin's Press, 2000): 3-4.

[13] Carter. *Mapping the Mind*; Fincher, J. *The Brain: Mystery of Matter and Mind* (Washington, DC: U.S. News & World Report Books, 1992); and Pribram, K.H. *Brain and Perception* (Hillsdale, NJ: Lawrence Erlbaum, 1991).

[14] Machado, L. *The Brain of the Brain* (Cidade do Cérebro, Brazil, 1990): 56-57.

[15] Restak, R. *The Secret Life of the Brain* (Washington, DC: National Academy Press, 2001): 128.

[16] Carter. *Mapping the Mind*; Fincher. *The Brain: Mystery of Matter and Mind*; and Pribram. *Brain and Perception*.

[17] See, for example: Cooper. *The Other 90%*.

[18] Drummond, Henry. *The Person Who Is Down* (New York: James Pott and Company, 1899).

[19] See, for example: Stoltz, P.G. *The Adversity Quotient* (New York: Wiley, 1997); and Stoltz, P.G. *The Adversity Quotient at Work* (New York: Morrow, 2000).

[20] Loehr, J.E. *Stress for Success* (New York: Times Books, 1997).

[21] Teich, M., and Dodeles, G. "Mind Control How to Get It, How to Use It, How to Keep It." Omni (Oct., 1987): 53-60; Miller, E.E. *Software for the Mind*

(Berkeley, CA: Celestial Arts, 1987); Otero, T.M. "Altering Your Inner Limits." in Sheikh, A.A. (Ed.) *Anthology of Imagery Techniques* (Milwaukee: American Imagery Institute, 1986): 289-311; Pribram, K.H. *Languages of the Brain* (New York: Brandon House, 1981). Wolpe, J. *The Practice of Behavior Therapy* (New York: Pergamin Press, 1973); Wolpe, J. *Life Without Fear: Anxiety and Its Cure* (Oakland, CA: New Harbinger, 1988).

[22]Star-performing individuals in many different fields use imagery and anchoring to toughen up and improve their chances of success in facing adversity. One of the best books by a leading researcher in this field is Loehr. *Stress for Success.*

[23]Roosevelt, E. *My Day* (New York: Da Capo Press, 2001).

[24]Restak. *Mozart's Brain and the Fighter Pilot.*

[25]Crum, T.F. *The Magic of Conflict* (New York: Simon and Schuster, 1987): 120.

[26]Ray, M., and Myers, R. *Creativity in Business* (New York: Doubleday, 1986): 48-49.

[27]Korem, J.K. *The Positive Power of Negative Thinking* (New York: Basic Books, 2001).

[28]See, for example: Aronson, E. "Self-Justification" in *The Social Animal* (San Francisco: W.H. Freeman, 1972); Cialdini, R.B. "Commitment and Consistency" in *Influence* (Glenview, IL: Scott, Foresman, 1988); and Pfeffer, J., and Sutton, R.I. *The Knowing-Doing Gap* (Boston: Harvard Business School Press, 2000).

[29]Pfeffer and Sutton. *The Knowing-Doing Gap.*

[30]See, for example: Thayer, R.E. *The Origin of Everyday Moods* (New York: Oxford University Press, 1997); and Loehr. *Stress for Success.*

[31]Gleick, G. *Faster* (New York: Pantheon, 1999).

[32]Mackay, D.M. *Behind the Eye* (Cambridge, MA: Basil Blackwell, 1991).

[33]A very insightful book by one of the leading researchers in this field is: Moore-Ede, M. *The Twenty-Four Hour Society* (Boston: Addison-Wesley, 1993).

[34]Moore-Ede. *The Twenty-Four Hour Society*: 53.

[35] Rossi, E.L. *The Twenty Minute Break* (New York: TarcherPutnam, 1991); Grandjean, E. *Fitting the Task* (New York: Taylor and Francis, 1988); Janaro, R.E., et al. "A Technical Note on Increasing Productivity Through Effective Rest Break Scheduling." *Industrial Management* 30(1)(Jan./Feb., 1988): 29-33.

[36] Fried, R. *The Breath Connection* (New York: Plenum, 1991); and Cailliet, R., and Gross, L. *The Rejuvenation Strategy* (New York: Doubleday, 1987).

[37] Schiffman, S. "The Use of Flavor to Enhance the Efficacy of Reducing Diets." *Hospital Practice* 21(7)(1986): 44H-44R; Quebec studies cited in Bricklin, M. (Ed.) *Prevention's Lose Weight Guidebook* (Emmaus, PA: Rodale Press, 1992): 64; Henry, C.J.K., and Emergy, B. "Effect of Spiced Food on Metabolic Rate." *Human Nutrition: Clinical Nutrition* 40C(1986): 165-168.

[38] See, for example: Restak. *Mozart's Brain and the Fighter Pilot.*

[39] For further details, see: Cooper, R.K., and Cooper, L. *Low-Fat Living* (Emmaus, PA: Rodale Books, 1997).

[40] Institute of HeartMath (14700 W. Park Ave., Boulder Creek, CA 95006, 408-338-8700); Rein, G., Atkinson, M., and McCraty, R. A "The Physiological and Psychological Effects of Compassion and Anger." *Journal of Advancement in Medicine* (1996); McCraty, R., Atkinson, M., and Tiller, W.A. "A New Electrophysiological Correlates Associated with Intentional Heart Focus." *Subtle Energies* 4(3)(1995): 251-268; McCraty, R., Tiller, W.A., and Atkinson, M. "The Effects of Emotions on Short Term Heart Rate Variability Using Power Spectrum Analysis." *American Journal of Cardiology* 76(14)(1995): 1089-1093.

[41] Quoted in Franck, F. (Ed.) *What Does It Mean to be Human?* (New York: St. Martin's Press, 2000): 3-4.

[42] For further details, see: Cooper. *The Other 90%.*

[43] Dienstbier, R.A. "Arousal and Physiological Toughness: Implications for Mental and Physical Health." *Psychological Review* 96(1)(1989): 84-100; Loehr. *Stress for Success.*

[44] Backer, T.E. "How Health Promotion Programs Can Enhance Creativity." In Klarreich, S.H. (Ed.) *Health and Fitness in the Workplace* (New York: Praeger, 1987): 325-337.

[45]Loehr. *Stress for Success*; Sinyor, D., et al. "Aerobic Fitness Level and Reactivity to Psychosocial Stress." *Psychosomatic Medicine* 45(1983): 205-217; Keller, S., and Seraganian, P. "Physical Fitness Level and Autonomic Reactivity to Psychosocial Stress." *Journal of Psychosomatic Research* 28(4)(1984): 279-287.

[46]Weiss, J.M., et al. "Effects of Chronic Exposure to Stressors on Avoidance-Escape Behavior and on Brain Epinephrine." *Psychosomatic Medicine* 37(1975): 522-533.

[47]*Ibid*.

[48]Loehr. *Stress for Success*.

[49]Loehr. *Stress for Success*.

[50]Cooper, R.K. *High Energy Living* (Emmaus, PA: Rodale Books, 2000); and Cooper and Cooper. *Low-Fat Living*.

[51]Daniels, L., and Worthingham, C. *Therapeutic Exercise for Body Alignment and Function* (Philadelphia: W.B. Saunders, 1977): 77; Yessis, M. "Kinesiology." *Muscle & Fitness* (Feb. 1985): 18-19 and 142.

[52]To learn more about abdominal exercises, see: Cooper, R.K. *Health & Fitness Excellence* (Boston: Houghton Mifflin, 1989) and Cooper and Cooper. *Low-Fat Living*.

[53]Clayton, G. *Hare Brain, Tortoise Mind* (Hopewell, NJ: Ecco Press, 1997).

[54]For a description of liming and its applications, see: Cooper. *The Other 90%*.

[55]Hauri, P., and Linde, S. *No More Sleepless Nights* (New York: Wiley, 1990).

[56]Dotto, L. *Losing Sleep: How Your Sleep Habits Affect Your Life* (New York: Morrow, 1990).

[57]See, for example: Prochaska, J.O., Norcross, J.C., and DiClemente, C.C. *Changing for Good* (New York: Morrow, 1994).

[58]Butler, R. "What Learners Want to Know." In Sansone, C., and Harackiewicz, J.M. (Eds.) *Intrinsic and Extrinsic Motivation* (San Diego: Academic Press, 2000): 161-194.

[59]Lazarus, R.S. *American Psychologist*, 30 (1975): 553-561; DeLongis, A., et al. "Relationship of Daily Hassles, Uplifts, and Major Life Events to Health Status."

Health Psychology 1 (1982): 119-136; Kanner, A.D., et al. "Comparison of Two Modes of Stress Measurement: Daily Hassles and Uplifts Versus Major Life Events." *Journal of Behavioral Medicine* 4 (1981): 1-39.

[60]See, for example: Wood, J., Matthews, A., and Dalgleish, T. "Anxiety and Cognitive Inhibition." *Emotion* 1(2)(2001): 166-181.

[61]Zillman, D. "Mental Control of Angry Aggression." In Wegner, D., and Pennebaker, J.S. (Eds.) *Handbook for Mental Control* (New York: Prentice Hall, 1993).

[62]Henriques, J., and Davidson, R. "Brain Electrical Asymmetries During Cognitive Task Performance in Depressed and Nondepressed Subjects." *Biological Pyschiatry* 42(1997): 1039-1050.

[63]See, for example: Stroebel, C.F. QR: *The Quieting Reflex* (New York: Berkley Books, 1983); and Sedlacek, K. *The Sedlacek Technique* (New York: McGraw-Hill, 1989).

[64]Hendler, S.S. *The Oxygen Breakthrough* (New York: Simon and Schuster, 1989).

[65]"Breathing Linked to Personality." *Psychology Today* (Jul., 1983): 109; Teich, M., and Dodeles, G. "Mind Control."

[66]Ekman, P., Levenson, R.W., and Friesen, W.V. "Autonomic Nervous System Activity Distinguishes Among Emotions." *Science* (Sep. 16, 1983): 1208-1210; Greden, J., et al. *Archives of General Psychiatry* 43 (1987): 269-274; Teich and Dodeles. "Mind Control"; Zajonc, R.B. "Emotion and Facial Efference: A Theory Reclaimed." *Science* 228 (4695)(Apr. 5, 1985): 15-21.

[67]Bloomfield, H.H., and Cooper, R.K. *Think Safe, Be Safe* (New York: Crown, 1995).

[68]Riskind, J.H., and Gotay, C.C. "Physical Posture: Could It Have Regulatory or Biofeedback Effects on Motivation and Emotion?" *Motivation and Emotion* 6 (3)(1982): 273-298.

[69]See, for example: Nadler, G., and Hibino, S. *Breakthrough Thinking* (Rocklin, CA: Prima Publishing, 1990); and Nadler, G., and Hibino, S., with Farrell, J. *Creative Solution Finding* (Rocklin, CA: Prima Publishing, 1995).

[70]Bargh, J.A., and Chartrand, T.L. "The Unbearable Automaticity of Being." *American Psychologist* 54(7)(1999): 462-479.

[71]Sheikh, A.A. *Imagery: Current Theory, Research, and Application.* (New York: Wiley, 1983).

[72]The classic inspirational book about tracking is *The Tracker*, by Tom Brown, Jr. (New York: Berkley Publishing, 1996); see also Halfpenny, J. *Field Guide to Mammal Tracking in North America* (Boulder, CO: Johnson Publishing, 1988).

[73]See, for example: Pribram. *Brain and Perception.*

[74]See, for example: Cooper. *The Other 90%*; and Cooper, R.K., and Sawaf, A. *Executive EQ: Emotional Intelligence in Leadership and Organizations* (New York: Grosset-Putnam, 1997).

[75]See: Jaques, E., and Cason, K. *Human Capability* (Falls Church, VA: Cason Hall, 1994); and Jaques, E. *Time-Span Handbook* (Falls Church, VA: Cason Hall, 1964).

[76]See, for example: Sansone, C., and Harackiewicz, J.M. (Eds.) *Intrinsic and Extrinsic Motivation* (New York: Academic Press, 2000); Hen, G., et al. "Examination of Relationships Among Trait-Like Individual Differences, State-Like Individual Differences, and Learning Performance." *Journal of Applied Psychology* 85(6)(2000): 835-847; and VandeWalle, D., et al. "The Influence of Goal Orientation and Self-Regulation Tactics on Sales Performance: A Longitudinal Field Test." *Journal of Applied Psychology* 84(2)(1999): 249-259.

[77]See, for example: Stockdale, J.B. *Courage Under Fire* (Stanford, CA: Hoover Institution: 1993, No. 6); Stockdale, J. and S. *In Love and War* (Annapolis, MD: Naval Institute Press, 1990); Wholey, D. *When the Worst That Can Happen Already Has* (New York: Hyperion, 1992); Cramer, K.D. *Staying on Top When Your World Turns Upside Down* (New York: Viking, 1990); Flach, F. *Resilience* (New York: Fawcett-Columbine, 1988); and Collins, J. *Good to Great* (New York: HarperBusiness, 2001).

[78]Cialdini, R. *The Psychology of Influence* (New York: Prentice Hall, 1993).

[79]See, for example: Diamond, M.C. *Enriching Heredity* (New York: Free Press, 1988); Montagu, A. *Growing Young* (New York: McGraw-Hill, 1988).

[80]O'Brian, P. *Picasso: A Biography* (New York: W.W. Norton, 1976).

[81]Galassi, S.G. *Picasso's One-Liners* (New York: Artisan Books, 1997).

[82]Holton, G. (Ed.) "Albert Einstein Autobiographical Notes." Translated by Schilpp, P.A. (Ed.) *Albert Einstein: Philosopher-Scientist* (Evanston, IL: Library of Living Philosophers, 1949); Erikson, J.M. *Wisdom and the Senses* (New York: Norton, 1988): 30-33.

[83]Born, M., and Franck, J. *Physiker in ihrer Zeit : der Luxus des Gewissens : Ausstellung der Staatsbibliothek* (Berlin, Stiftung Preussischer Kulturbesitz, 1958).

[84]See, for example: De Bono, E. *Serious Creativity* (New York: HarperBusiness, 1992).

[85]Provine, R. *Laughter: A Scientific Investigation* (New York: Viking, 2002).

[86]Sala, F. "Relationship Between Executives' Spontaneous Use of Humor and Effective Leadership." (Ph.D. dissertation, Boston University Graduate School of Arts and Science, 2000).

[87]Mintzberg, H. *The Rise and Fall of Strategic Planning* (News York: Free Press, 1994).

[88]Selye, H. *The Stress of Life* (New York: McGraw-Hill, 1956).

[89]King-Hele, D. *Erasmus Darwin* (London: Giles de la Mare, 2000).

[90]See, for example: Horn, J. "Models of Intelligence." In Linn, R. (Ed.) *Intelligence* (Chicago: University of Illinois Press, 1989): 29-73; Horn, J., and Cattell, R.B. "Refinement and Test of Fluid and Crystallized Intelligence." *Journal of Educational Psychology* 57(1966): 253-270.

[91]Baldwin. *Edison: Inventing the Century* (New York: Hyperion, 1995).

[92]See, for example: Diamond. *Enriching Heredity;* and Montagu. *Growing Young.*

[93]Patton, G. In Charlton, J. (Ed.) *The Military Quotation Book* (New York: St. Martin's Press, 2002).

[94]Baldwin. *Edison: Inventing the Century.*

[95]Bandura, A. *The Principles of Behavior Modification* (New York: Holt, Reinhart, 1969); and Bandura, A. "Self-Efficacy: Toward a Unifying Theory of Behavioral Change." *Psychological Review* 84(1977): 191-215.

[96]One example is: Wholey. *When the Worst That Can Happen Already Has.*

[97]Tice, D. Study results reported in *The New York Times* (Dec. 30, 1992: C6).

[98]Eliot, R.S., and Breo, D.L. *Is It Worth Dying For?* (New York: Bantam, 1989).

[99]Pennebaker, J.W., Kiecolt-Glaser, J.K., and Glaser, R. "Disclosure of Traumas and Immune Function." *Journal of Consulting and Clinical Psychology* 56(1988): 239-245.

[100]Peterson, K.S. "To Fight Stress, Women Talk, Men Walk." *USA Today* Aug. 7, 2000: D1.; Taylor, S., et al. *Psychological Review* (Autumn, 2000).

[101]Land, G. *Grow or Die: The Unifying Principle of Transformation* (New York: Wiley, 1986): 9.

[102]Old notes carved in rock near Chonggye, in Central Tibet.

[103]Sun Tzu II information drawn from: Cleary, T. (Trans.) *The Lost Art of War by Sun Tzu II* (New York: HarperCollins, 1996); von Senger, H. *The Book of Stratagems* (New York: Viking, 1991); and Lau, D.C., and Ames, R.T. (Trans.) *Sun Pin: The Art of Warfare* (New York: Ballantine, 1996).

[104]Cited in Cleary, T. (Trans.) *Sun Tzu: The Art of War* (Boston: Shambhala, 1988).

[105]"The Master of Demon Valley." In Cleary, T. *Thunder in the Sky: On the Acquisition and Exercise of Power* (Boston: Shambhala, 1993).

[106]Ji, L. In Cleary, T. *Mastering the Art of War* (Boston: Shambhala, 1989): 96-98.

Excelerating

About the Author

Praised as "a national treasure" by Stanford Business School Professor Michael Ray and named "the ultimate business guru for the new millennium" by *USA Today*, for five straight years Robert Cooper was the highest-rated faculty member in the Lessons in Leadership Distinguished Speaker Series® sponsored by universities and business schools nationwide. In May 2002, Dr. Cooper launched his new Breakthroughs in Leadership Series™ from coast to coast.

An acclaimed educator on how exceptional leaders and teams can apply today's scientific breakthroughs to liberate untapped human capacities and excel under pressure, Cooper is also recognized for his pioneering work on the practical application of emotional intelligence and the neuroscience of trust and leadership.

In his life he has been a newspaper delivery boy, housepainter, farm worker, martial artist, All-American athlete, U.S. Marine, rock climber, carpenter, surveyor, university honor student, independent scholar, wilderness survival instructor, newspaper columnist, health and fitness instructor, co-developer of measurement systems on peak performance and emotional intelligence, chair of the board for a metrics firm specializing in leadership advancement and applied intelligence, consultant to a global high-technology consortium, advisor to organizational leaders, and a public speaker. He has learned from scientists, inventors, teachers, refugees, star performers in many fields, and people in all walks of life.

In a recent survey of managers and professionals from more than 90 organizations, his work was compared to twenty other widely recognized leadership authorities, and Cooper rated highest on every scale, including inherent value, usefulness, applicability, delivery, and overall results. In an independent rating by managers and professionals in the Senior Management Interchange, the value of his work was rated at 4.9 out of 5.0.

Dr. Cooper's practical advice has garnered accolades from all quarters. His articles have been published in Strategy & Leadership, and his books, including *The Performance Edge* and *Executive EQ: Emotional Intelligence in Leadership & Organizations*, have sold over four million copies. His recent book, *The Other 90%: How to Unlock Your Vast Untapped Potential for Leadership and Life* (Crown Business), received 5-star reviews and has been on *The Wall Street Journal* and *Business Week* Bestseller Lists, and #3 on Amazon's Top 100 List.

He serves as Adjunct Professor in the Ph.D. Program at the Union Institute and University in Cincinnati. In addition to graduate work at the University of Michigan and University of Iowa, he completed his undergraduate degree with honors at the University of Minnesota and earned his doctorate at the Union Institute and University Graduate College in health and psychology with an emphasis on leadership.

Cooper serves as chair of Advanced Excellence Systems LLC, a leadership consulting firm in Ann Arbor, MI. He has designed and presented leadership development and professional education programs for many organizations, including 3M, Verizon, American Express, Hilton, Disney, Ford, Morgan Stanley, Sun Microsystems, Marriott, American Chamber of Commerce Executives, Concours, Management Centre Europe, Novartis, Georgia-Pacific, J.D. Edwards, GlaxoSmithKline, Guinness, Scientific-Atlanta, Delta Air Lines, Fidelity Investments, Ball

Aerospace, PNC Bank, Methodist Hospitals of Dallas, American Hospital Association, Deloitte & Touche, Booz/Allen/Hamilton, Children's Healthcare of Atlanta, Department of Veterans Affairs, Department of the Interior, Social Security Administration, Fireman's Fund Insurance, Qualcomm, Andersen, Northwestern Mutual Life, The Limited, Allstate Insurance, and Coca-Cola.

Beyond his corporate work, Cooper's background includes a decade of study on stress dynamics, change management, health sciences and psychology, and he has earned instructor-level certifications from several leading preventive medicine institutions. He served in the U.S. Marine Corps during the Vietnam War. An All-American athlete, he is a recipient of the University of Michigan's Honor Trophy Award for "outstanding achievement in scholarship, athletics, and leadership." He lives in Ann Arbor, Michigan, with his wife and children.

Share Excelerating

To order additional signed copies of the book, inquire about quantity discounts, or learn about Robert Cooper's seminars, consulting, coaching and other products and services:

Telephone: Toll-Free (877) 709-9775 or (515) 278-1700
E-mail: Cooper@RobertKCooper.com
Web Site: www.RobertKCooper.com

Sign up today to receive your free copy of our new e-mail newsletter:

"Strategies for Excelling in a Changing World"

This newsletter presents Robert's latest insights on bringing out more of the best in yourself and others—plus special discounts on his forthcoming books, seminars, audio and video programs, and more. To sign up today, please send us your name, organization, street address, and e-mail address. You can contact us by phone, e-mail, or by visiting our web site.

Join us in...
Making a greater difference.
Excelling in a changing world.
Doing it now.